AS IT WAS IN THE DAYS OF NOAH!

The Noah Prophecy

Connecting Noah's cataclysmic event days
to the coming End-Times events!

By

Dr. S. Asher

AS IT WAS IN THE DAYS OF NOAH
THE NOAH PROPHECY

Copyright © 2019
PUBLISHED BY KDP 2019
Edited by MJS. LTD

CONTACT – INFO@AHLCglobal.com

ALL RIGHTS RESERVED. NO PART OF THIS PUBLICATION MAY BE REPRODUCED, STORED IN A RETRIEVAL SYSTEM, OR TRANSMITTED IN ANY FORM OR BY ANY MEANS, ELECTRONIC, MECHANICAL, PHOTOCOPY, RECORDING OR OTHERWISE, WITHOUT THE PRIOR PERMISSION OF THE COPYRIGHT OWNER.

PRINTED IN THE UNITED STATES OF AMERICA
ISBN: 9781092539623

Printed in the USA by Amazon Books

Contents

About this book	
Sealed, Saved & Tormented	Pg-1
Daniel's prophesied days:	
1260th Day	Pg-2
1275th Day	Pg-6
1290th Day	Pg-12
1335th Day	Pg-13
The Scorpions – The Shayatim-Jinn	Pg-15
The Sign of Jonah	Pg-23
End to Captivity in New Egypt	Pg-30
Exodus-16, The Quail & Mannah	Pg-37
Appendix-A	Pg-51
First Warning	Pg-51
Second Warning	Pg-62
Third Warning	Pg-72
Fourth Warning	Pg-87
Fifth Warning	Pg-95
Sixth Warning	Pg-100
Joel-Sixth Warning Part-2	Pg-108
Seventh Warning	Pg-114
Beacon-Seed excerpt	Pg-123
About the Author	Pg-132
Bibliography	Pg-134
Other Works	Pg-135

About this book

This book is meant to realign a person's understanding of some highly significant Hebrew prophecies for the end days. In doing so, it will continue to prove the utter importance for all souls to *Return* to the Eternal Creators original, 1st law path.

If you remain unaware of the 1st law of the Everlasting Agreement, please read – *The Land of Meat & Honey* - (Asher); since understanding the more accurate details of these prophets means little without *Returning* to that original path.

As it was in the days of Enoch and Noah; and as it was later reiterated to Abrahim, to Moshe, and later taught by the Essene Master and prophet, Yehshua, is most likely the most important prophetic understanding anyone can have, but one that so few actually have correct.

Additionally, herein you will find seven *warnings* received but reluctantly made public from 2015 to 2019. Few have seen all seven which is why I am publishing them in this book. The latest warning, and the one I tend to believe to be the final warning, of 2019, was the final impetus for compiling it all here as an expanded understanding of the Creator's calendar.

This book is better understood when used side by side with the Creator's Calendar guide book which can be found at www.AHLCglobal.com or at Amazon books by that title and under the author's name. If you do not yet have Dr. Asher's Creator's calendar guide, now would be a good time to have one on hand.

The Sealed, The Saved, and the Tormented

Jer 11:11 *"¹¹ Therefore thus says Yehovah; 'Behold, I will bring destruction upon them which they will not escape; and though they will cry out to me, I will not attend to them!"*

How important is having the exact, original Creator's Calendar system, knowing it and following it without fail? As I have said previously in podcasts on this calendar topic, this is a question that I have received many times in the last few years, but my answer to it, and the import of it has expanded exponentially as we near the edge of the abyss of this world.

Following, I will be going into the books of Daniel, Revelation primarily; as well as making references to some New Testament verses you may know. However, the references I will use are by far not all that exists in the Tanak and most likely in the NT, on this topic. I will also say, this may be one of the most important contemporary topics that I will be teaching on other than the Everlasting Agreement, itself.

Additionally, what you are about to hear will contrast greatly to pretty much all of the prophecy detail you have ever heard taught concerning Daniel, Ezekiel, and Revelation.

If you have my calendar book or the calendar itself that was created by Mr. Barry Usher, then have them on hand for reference. As this will begin to show how virtually all Hebrew prophecy is aligned and correlated with the Creator's Calendar system, and how

NO prophecy can be understood at all outside of this calendar system.

Let's begin by correlating what the great prophet Dani'el said regarding specific days on the calendar:

1260-days: Month of Asher, on the 8th day in 2017-aka-[Aug/21] the 2600-year Age period ended, leaving the sign of the *fish-Pisces* and entering the sign of enlightenment-*Aquarius*. That date was also our warning sign for the coming 7-year Shmitah countdown which we are in now.

- Will this be the final countdown to the end, and renewed beginning?
- Will the next sign of Jonah, *the eclipse over the USA again on*

    April/8/2024 be our second sign alerting us to the end of Yehovah's great judgment exercise for this place?

Yes, I do believe this will be the time and our *sign* of exactly that, and much more.

- We have one SIGN to alert us to the beginning countdown;
- And we get the 2nd SIGN alerting His people that all hostilities

    have ended.

This is the way I have come to understand these two signs.

As stated previously, on the 15th day of Asher, we have the 1260th day of Daniel, and this is directly associated with Yohannan's Revelation of chapter-11:

Rev 11:1 *"And a reed like a staff was given to me, and the angel stood, saying; '<u>Arise and measure the temple</u> [people] <u>of God, and the altar, and those worshiping in it</u>."*

NOTE: Is the "alter" of The Eternal One on earth? **No!** His altar was created on the 4th day and has remained unmolested since then above our heads – **The Sun and the Stars.** The Moon was added later!

Moreover, what is an "altar" by Hebrew definition and culture? It is a "PILLAR!" And what is a "pillar" if not a very important FOUNDATION or "foundational" support point? A foundational structure like maybe, *the entire system of constellations* above us which MUST connect with and synchronize into His original calendar system? Yohannan (John) was told to measure/count the SEALED ones of the Eternal One just as the three Malakim were told to do during Jeremiah's time prior to being released from Jerusalem which was under siege for over a year. And as I have shown in my books, those who were MARKED on their heads with <u>His name</u> in Jerusalem, by those Messengers, on that day, and soon, here again, were those who refused to murder and eat the flesh of their neighbors! THIS IS RECORDED FACT.

Yohannan Measures the Lawless

11:2 *"And <u>leave out</u> the exterior court of the temple, and <u>do not measure it</u>. For it was given to the lawless, and they will trample the holy city <u>forty-two months</u>* – [1260-days]. *3 And I will give to my two witnesses, and they will prophesy a thousand, two hundred and sixty days, dressed in sackcloth. 4 These are the two olive trees, and the two lampstands, standing before the Creator of the earth."*

The "exterior court" is known to us as the "Court of the Gentiles." To the later *Shelanite-Judah* understanding, this would, of course, be

all souls who are NOT them, because those people do not follow *their* law. They are believed to be the great unwashed animals of humanity, however, that is not the truth of it since *their* altars, *their* temples, *their* courts, *their* sabbaths, *their* feasts, *their* new moons, and festivals ARE NOT HIS! He has been very clear to advise them that
He HATES everything about them, to include their many prayers and songs. So then, quite obviously this is all prophesying about something else.

Yohannan of Revelation fame is being told to both, measure/COUNT the *Righteous-Yeshurim* first, and then clearly instructs him to have no regard for counting the LAWLESS ones who chose to live outside of HIS temple, of HIS law. AND, now if you refer to my – <u>Warning of 3 Years</u> – in the back of this book, you will then understand just how bad it is about to become for all those who have remained, by their own consent, outside as lawless.

NOTE: The two witnesses are not and will never be Christian. They were and are still Hebrew men, prophets who will be warning everyone "outside in the court of the Gentiles" what is coming, but most importantly HOW to exclude themselves from it. They will most certainly be telling everyone to **Return** to the Eternal One's <u>1st law</u>, which is established in His <u>Everlasting Agreement</u>.

The two witnesses of Revelation 11 are not who the Christian sects believe them to be. This point was shown to me many years ago and after carefully studying the connections, for me, it is sufficiently proven through the texts of Daniel and Revelation. It is clear and simple, and we all know how much I like simple; because if it isn't simple and easy to find and SEE, it's the lie.

It has always been quite obvious to me that the same violence that was done to my own Hebrew texts by the scribes, was the same violence that the original words of Yehshua and his taught ones received equally. So know this, whatever the later Hellenized stories of Yehshua's original teachings and words received, they most definitely received the additional coloring of *Stupid-stitions.* One of those superstitions was the inclusion that everyone back then was speaking directly to either some "god" in the flesh or some "angel."

When you see the man Yohannan receiving prophetic messages from what most believe to be Yehshua or an angel, you should be harkened back to another prophet who was told that he would get back to certain parts of his vision-instructions at a later date. But, you should also recall that this other, more ancient prophet (*who, by the scriptures, we know for a certainty that he lived by the 1st law of the Everlasting Agreement*) was also instructed to "shut up" certain parts, received.

Of course, that man was Daniel. And it was Daniel, NOT Yehshua or some other "angel" who was used to finally unseal that which was shut up for so long. **Daniel was sent to Yohannan!**

Dan 12:4 *"But you, Dani'el, shut up the words and seal the book to the end-time. Many will travel in and out, and knowledge will be increased."*

[I believe "Travel in & out" is referring to the Soul recycling system]

Dan 12:13 *"But you go on **to the end**, for you will rest – [Die], and then stand-[Live] for your work at the end of days."*

Thus, it will be Daniel and Yohannan who will be the two witnesses as depicted in Revelation, and NOT Moshe and Elijeh as I have generally believed it would be.

The Malakim Seal their Foreheads

Rev 7:3 *"Do not harm the ground, nor the sea, nor the trees, until we seal the servants of the Eternal One on their foreheads."*

Rev 7:4 *"And I heard the number of those having <u>been sealed</u>: one hundred forty-four thousand, having <u>been sealed</u> out of every tribe of the sons of Jacob:"*

Throughout every single biblical event where His "Upright ones" the "Yeshurim" were intermingled with the greater majority of Chaff who had to be burned out, always came the instruction to His Malakim to MARK and SEAL His name on their foreheads. <u>*It is the SEAL of understanding & obedience!*</u>

Example: I personally understand the 1st law of His Everlasting Agreement, and thus, by understanding, which is now MARKED on my forehead - (what I know) - and proven out in my life by my Right Hand – (what I do), I have been SEALED! And thus, I am now privy to much deeper knowledge and understanding which is hidden to most, and I have all the prophesied protections and provisions bestowed upon me when required. Those who remain outside in the *court of the Gentiles* in which Yohannan was told to ignore, *not so much.* Outside of the 1st law of His Everlasting Agreement as prophesied and lined out by Noah and the Eternal One's many prophets in all Ages, there is no other *Mark* or *Seal* of AHEEYEH! There can be only one.

1275-Days: Month of Asher, 30th day: Beginning of Final Calamities!

Rev-10:10 *"And I took the little scroll out of* [Daniel's]*hand, and devoured it. And it was sweet like honey in my mouth; and when I ate it, my belly was made bitter.* [I removed the word, Angel.]

Rev 10:11 *"And he* [Daniel] *said to me; 'You must <u>again</u> prophesy <u>before peoples</u> and <u>nations</u> and <u>tongues</u> and <u>many kings</u>.'*

==When did Yohannan ever do any of this stuff as stated there?== This is all still to come, and he will be speaking, prophesying to their faces in the streets, and as it is written, all eyes will see, and he won't be alone doing it. Yohannan is one of the two witnesses, and Daniel will be along for that ride.

NOTE: Is it difficult to understand that Yohannan, at that time, did not actually know the ancient prophet Daniel by sight? Is it difficult to understand that Yohannan may not have received the bigger picture to come and his extended part in it at the end of days until he left this plane of existence, and was told? Part of John's data was for us, the rest he will receive later when his time comes.

But why are they coming again? It tells you why! For them to "Prophesy" to everyone on CNN, NBC, MSNBC, FOX, etc., that this short period of time *(at that time <u>and on our calendar</u>)* will be the last minutes given for them to make ***Teshuvah*** and leave their cities. And as the story goes, we all know how that turns out for the two witnesses, right? They are killed because a majority of people CONSENT and CHOOSE to murder and ALLOW them to be murdered and left to rot in those streets. And THAT was exactly meant to be the FINAL answer on this game show!

Dan 12:8 *"And I heard, but did not understand. And I said, my Elohim, what will be the end of these things? 9 And He said; 'Go, Daniel! For the words are closed up and sealed <u>until the end time</u>. 10 Many will be purified and made clean through testing. But the wicked will do evil. And <u>not one</u> of the wicked will understand, <u>but the wise will</u> understand."*

12:11 *"And from the time the regular* ==sacrifice== *is <u>eschewed</u>, and the abomination that desolates <u>adapted</u>, 1290-days will occur."*

Major points of contention with the previous text. First; They ADDED the word **"sacrifice"** in there. It is NOT in the Hebrew text nor is it the context here. This has given birth to some major lies and misdirection! *Second;* I changed two words although I can change them all too far better English words to represent the Hebrew more accurately, but, these get us there. First, understand that they removed whatever Hebrew word was there before adding "Sacrifice."

So, with the added word removed, read it like this –

12:11 *"And from the time the regular* [missing word] *is* eschewed, *and the abomination that desolates* adapted, *1290-days will pass."*

The other words – *eschewed* **and** *adapted* – are far more accurate with the original context, which is 100% about prayer! Oh yes, something was "usurped" via their false religion narratives back then and it has never been remedied yet since, but added to. AND, if we understand these texts correctly and prophetically, we can be assured that the next time this issue of the [missing word] comes alive again, it will undoubtedly affect your spiritual walk with the Creator, and most surely concerning the *days* and *times* that you take those walks.

Because in those end-times as it was specifically and obviously expressed to Daniel to fall on, someone up high in world power will attempt to openly change or remove our ability to pray, identically as the King did during Daniel's time.

The RCC and the Shelanite-Sanhedrin-Jews, as of March 2019, have made some compact that is yet fully known. What is suggested at this time is that they plan to force their SUN-day law on everyone who is not already a proven Orthodox Jew. All will be subject to their false "Noahide laws" with the acceptation of all orthodox Jews. And, anyone found keeping anything in their lives even remotely similar to Torah will be arrested and killed for it. THAT much is already in their laws.

Now, based on the actual context of the entire story, and with the RE-addition of the original word they removed, read it like this –

"And from the time the daily <u>prayer</u> is <u>eschewed</u>, and the abomination that desolates <u>adapted</u>, 1290-days will pass."
[There it is! Only took 3500 years to reestablish it.]
So, the Abomination of Desolation is NOT a man or Satan or a statue of the Pope, or a pig that they roasted in the Temple. It was and remains the changing of, or outright revocation of our prayer times, whatever they may be, (Sun-up / Noon & and or late afternoon), WHO we make those prayers to, and making illegal (for us) all versions of all the 7 Jewish holidays (on their Hillel calendar), and all Sabbath's, along with whatever else they try to enforce along those lines, THAT WAS and WILL BE again the *Abomination that desolates. Why?* Because they changed, through the removal of Hebrew words and the manipulation of many more, *the:*

- *Prayer;*
- *The true NAME of the ONE we are to consult in prayer;*
- *His law which is the ONLY thing that makes us clean enough to go before him in the first place;*
- *And, His specific memorial days to do it on!*

Dan 6:5 *"Then these priests of Darius said; "We will not find any occasion against this Daniel unless we discover something against him <u>concerning the Law of his God</u>".*

OH REALLY! And what Law did Daniel keep? We already confirmed through the texts that Daniel was a serious vegetarian. We know he was serious because instead of going along with the King and his men on another occasion concerning the Kings choices of foods, *and unlike what the 99.9% will always do,* Daniel decided to teach the king and everyone else a better way, and later got big Kudos for it. – "*....* **unless we discover something against him concerning the Law of his God**".

Dan 6:7 *"All the presidents of the kingdom, the prefects, and the priests, the officials and the governors, planned together to establish a royal statute, and to make a firm decree that whoever will petition any god or man for thirty days, except from you, O king, he will be thrown into the den of lions."*

6:8 *"Now, O king, establish the decree and sign the document, so that it may not be changed, according to the law of the Medes and Persians, which does not pass away."*

6:9 *"All on account of this, King Darius signed the document and the decree."*

6:10 *"And when he had learned that the document was signed, Daniel went to his house. His windows were open in his upper room toward Jerusalem. He knelt on his knees* **three times in the day***, and prayed and praised before his the Eternal One, as he did before."*

So, Daniel flat out made a point to *openly* break this law as quickly as he could! What we see here is the 30-day trial of *the abomination that makes all things desolate* because *clean* prayer has ceased, and the prayers of even one Righteous Yehshurim – *Daniel* - hung in the balance. I assure you, not one other alleged "righteous" Vegan person prayed that day, or for the entire 30-days.

"And when he had opened the seventh seal, there was silence in heaven for the span of about 30 minutes"

And now you finally understand what one of the 7-Seals is! At this end-time, after the righteous are counted and the unrighteous ignored having made their final decision – ***Meneh-Meneh-Tikel-Upharsin*** – and after trying to silence His people and then temporarily silencing the two witness' - *Daniel and Yohannan,* then their final destruction will come. All of them and their wives and their children will be cut down like grass, dried, and ground down to dust, just as Isaiah prophesied, and exactly as we also see pictured in Daniel.

Dan 6:20 *"And when he came to the den, he cried with a grieved voice to Daniel. The king yelling, said to Daniel, O Daniel, servant of the living God, your God whom you always serve, is He able to deliver you from the lions? 21 Then Daniel said to the king, O king, live forever."*

Dan 6:22 *"My God has sent His Angel, and He has shut the mouths of the lions. And they have not harmed me, because in His sight innocence was found in me. And also before you, O king, I have done no harm."*

Dan 6:23 *"Then the king was exceedingly glad over him. And he commanded to bring up Daniel from the den. And Daniel was brought out of the den, <u>and no harm was found on him because he trusted in his God</u>."*

6:24 *"And the king commanded, <u>and they brought those men who had accused Daniel</u>. And <u>they threw them into the lions' den, them, their sons and their wives</u>. And the lions overpowered them and crushed all their bones before they reached to the bottom of the den."*

So look at this micro-account of heroic obedience and salvation through it, and take note of who King Darius, held in contempt and liable in the end. But, who put the hooks in those evil men's minds, hearts, and jaws? Who is the overall mighty one who is closer in proximity to us here? As you will see throughout the Jonah warnings from 2015 to this past week of 3/21/2019, it is always the mighty one Yehovah meting out the punishment to those who ***willingly choose*** evil.

And now when we reconsult this most recent ***"warning of the 3-years,"*** we understand that it will be Yehovah again. And by the prophetic end-times warnings of Isaiah, we clearly see that those punished in the end days are held accountable just as we saw they were during Daniel's time.

*"And the king commanded, <u>and they brought **those men** who had accused Daniel</u>. And <u>they threw them into the lions' den and **their sons** and **their wives** with them!</u> And the lions overpowered them and crushed all their bones before they reached to the bottom of the den."*

AND THAT will begin on the 1275th day – On the 30th Day in the month of Asher. Now, again, refer to my Warning of 3 Years:

Quick review:

- On the 15th of Asher (in that year); comes the final measurement/counting. It would be better to be living inside the 1st Law at that time.
- By the 30th of Asher, the stage is set, and the dogs of destruction are loosed on the world. There is an additional short time of mercy for others still outside in *the court,* to come in with us.
- Levi-15 is the (FINAL Ingathering feast of the Yeshurim). Much better to have made *Teshuvah-Returned*, by this time.
- From Levi-15 we count another 45-days to the 1335th day of Daniel. This 45-days is the final period of mercy for all outsiders to come in. After that, it's chaff burning time.

12:12 *"Blessed is he who waits and comes to the thousand, three hundred and thirty-five day."*

==1290-Days:== Levi-15: The Final festival of Ingathering! SHOULD HAVE ENTERED THE ARK by now!

From this point forward those <u>outside of the Ark of the Everlasting Agreement</u> who may still be redeemable and made up of those called the *Elect* and the *mixed multitude* will quickly begin to get the message from all the goings-on around them. How will they know what to do and where to go to find *the Hebrew's who* <u>KNOW God</u>, *as the prophets said?* They will have already been told by the two Witnesses' via the mass media but ignored their warnings of imminent destruction, and how to escape it. They went along with the 99.9%.

Yehovah, *as described in the Isaiah 3-year warning prophecies*, has now begun to bring utter destruction on everyone remaining outside.

My understanding from what the prophets put forth is that the bad times will begin and grow in intensity, but still escapable to those who decide to "believe" and "consent" to the previously instructed life changes. Blessed are those who make the decision to join us before the 1335th day, and before the final door slams shut.

Dan = The Judge - Final Judgment – Sign of Scorpio – Scorpions Sting for 5-Months!

The 1335th day is the 30th day in the month of Dan. It is also the <u>Sabbath day</u> AND, <u>in the winter</u>! *Ring any bells?*

After the 1335th day will begin the 5-months of men's' torment by the alleged sting from some mythical scorpions or alleged alien invasion, the ideas taken from these prophecies of Daniel and Revelation have run the gamut because no one has understood their true and most simple meanings; which are direct references to the original Creator's calendar system as lined out originally IN THE DAYS OF NOAH!

As I have mentioned in other teachings, I tend to believe that this "torment" from *scorpions*, or more accurately from the "time of" *Scorpio-Dan*, will NOT be some physical manmade or alien weapon that attacks them physically. It, however, appears that they will be attacked "mentally," and playing out in various, horrific ways. Our best visual on this from Holly-wood may be from the 2018 Sandra Bullock movie titled "Bird-Box." Where *Jinn* like entities overtook peoples minds, made them instantly insane killing themselves and others. The most intriguing part of it, and how I see it directly connecting to our prophecies as you will see explained in more detail later in this book, is that *only the people who went outside of their homes or buildings* became affected, overcome and lost in that movie.

This is exactly what several of our prophets have warned about, and also exactly as I have taught in connection with how the Sabbath day quarantine command came into effect during Moshe's time. And how since then has never been rescinded, but always ignored. Believe me, that single point of law will come into play someday soon and take the small remnant of even the righteous down to a remnant of a remnant. Mark my words.

Recapping WHY they will be tormented and how?

Simply, because they decided to CONSENT to remain in their evil, which is literally everything, both seemingly benign acts to outright unlawful acts and edicts of every kind known to man or beast that most have always taken for granted, or truly embraced as evil. And, their final decision on this was made AFTER hearing the path of their potential reprieve via the two witnesses! (To Return to the 1st law!)

They delighted in the removal of two most righteous individuals! And for this they received….:

2Th 2:10 *"…and in all deceitfulness of the unrighteousness in those killed, because the love of the truth was not embraced by them to be saved, 11 because of this will Yehovah send to them a strong delusion, for* _choosing_ the lie, 12 _that they may be judged—all who did not believe the truth,_ [via two witnesses] _but were satisfied in their unrighteousness."_

Remember the Giants from Enoch's texts? Recall how they were killed off? Enoch was told to relay the orders of their fate from the Eternal One, which came down through the "overlord – mighty one" Yehovah who is the one who meted out that justice AFTER those giants, who were the offspring of angels and women, broke the 1st law of the Everlasting Agreement. They were allowed to exist right up until they began eating all the animals, and people.

Their fate - Somehow Yehovah caused them to fight one another until they all killed each other off completely. And their angelic parents were made to watch it all happen. Additionally, their souls were never going to be allowed back into heaven, but locked here within the confines of this earth, forever. It appears those giants as well were sent some "strong delusion" which made them go insane, and by the exact same entity who all of our prophetic texts say will be in charge of doing it all over again to the majority of mankind.

Round-2 - Revelation begins on the last day of the month of Dan!

The Shayatim – _Jinn_ - The Scorpion unleashed!

Rev 9:3 _"And out of the smoke locusts came forth to the earth. And_ authority was given _to them,_ as the **scorpions** _of the earth_ have authority._"_

9:4 _"And it was said to them that they should not harm the_ grass _of the earth,_ nor every green _thing,_ nor every tree, **except only** the people who do not have the seal of God on their foreheads._"_

9:5 _"And it was told to them that they_ should not kill them, _but that they_ **are tormented five months**. _And their torment_ **is as** _the torment of a_ scorpion when it stings a man._"_

9:6 *"And in those days men will seek death, and they will not find it. And they will long to die, yet death will flee from them."*

Eze 1:4 *"And I looked, and, saw a whirlwind coming from the north, <u>a great cloud of fire enfolding itself</u>, <u>very bright</u> was it, and out of the middle was the color of <u>amber from the middle of the fire</u>. 5 Also out of the middle came <u>the likeness</u> of four living creatures. And this was their appearance; <u>they had the likeness of a man</u>.* [The Shayatim Jinn]
1:6 *"And every one had four faces, and every one had four wings. 7 And their feet were straight feet, and the sole of their feet was like the sole of a calf's foot: and they sparkled like the color of bright brass. 8 And they had the hands of a man under their wings on four sides; they four faces and wings. 9 Their wings were joined one to another; they turned not when they flew and all went straight forward. 10 As for the likeness of their faces, all four had the face of a man and the face of a lion. On the right side they four; the face of an ox on the left side; and all four also had the face of an eagle. 11 Thus was their faces. Their wings were stretched upward; two wings of every one were joined one to another, and two covered their bodies. 12 And they moved every one straight forward: <u>As a soul moves, they went</u>; and they turned not when they went. 13 As for the likeness of the living creatures, <u>their appearance was like burning coals of fire</u>, like <u>the appearance of light</u>: It went up and down among the living creatures, and <u>the fire was bright</u>, <u>and out of the fire went out lightning</u>. 14 And the living creatures moved away and returned <u>as the appearance of a flash of lightning</u>."*

The "Shayatim" are the "evil" *Jinn*.

Ancients believed that the Creator, created three sets of life:

- *The Sefirot – <u>Varying levels of Angels of light;</u>*

- *The souls of man which projected the Eternal's light before being covered with "skins."*
- And, the Jinn which was created with fire.

<u>THIS is exactly what Ezekiel saw and described</u>.

It is believed from ancient times to this day that most Jinn protect man from the few who are against man and the Creator. In the Muslim tradition, it is believed that the evil Jinn will be released in the end times to destroy mankind. They are known to get inside a person's mind to destroy from within, and they can take any physical or non-physical form or likeness. If you read the Ezekiel account very carefully, see how they move, like *lightning, like wind, like ghosts*. Exactly as described will happen in many end-times prophecies, but most generally misunderstood as such through the later Jewish and Christian dogmas. And most certainly by design.

Dan = The Judge - Final Judgment begins on the 1335th day – 30th day of Dan – Sign of Scorpio for 5-Months!

"...And <u>authority was given</u> to them, **as** the **<u>scorpions</u>** of the earth <u>have authority</u>.

"As" the scorpions of the earth – NOT "by" the scorpions of the earth, or giant bugs from outside of the earth!

".... And their torment **<u>is as</u>** <u>the torment of a scorpion when it stings a man</u>" - ["is as" or "like"].

".... And it was said to them that they should not harm the <u>grass</u> of the earth, <u>nor every green</u> thing, <u>nor every tree</u>, **except only** <u>the people who do not have the seal of God on their foreheads</u>."

Staying with the local context here, this previous line is speaking directly about "people", not shrubbery!

The *grass*, *green thing*, every *tree*, etc., is allegorical for *"the righteous people!"* NOT nature in general. It does not just change context from grass and trees in the same breath as wiping out the unrighteous **people** who have no Seal.

Be Sealed BEFORE the 1335th day, or be destroyed by the *Shayatim* in some horrific way.

Timing is everything!

AS IT WAS IN THE DAYS OF NOAH…!

Five months of torment beginning at the end of Dan brings us to the Noah flood event timing again of more than one year! Right at 1-year and 1 month give or take.

Rev 9:15 *"And the four angels were released, those having been prepared for the **hour** and **day** and **month** and **year**, that they should kill the third part of men."*

Break that down in reverse: 1-**Year**, and 1-**month**, a day and an hour! *Exactly as the complete Noah catastrophe cycle occurred!*

When it states - ***A day and an hour*** - That is a lot unlike when the texts say – ***As the wages of a man***. It is there to depict absolute specificity. That this **Year** and **Month** will begin and end at specific times. As it was in the days of Noah!

More importantly, is that it lands us in the month of "Salvation!" NEFTALI! Which is ruled by the sign known as the LAMB, a small constellation in the shape of a Shepherds' staff.

From the 30th day of Dan, which is a Sabbath day, *and*, in the winter, and by moving through 5-months from Dan-30 (the 1335th day) we are landed on the 27th day of NEFTALI! Just like with Noah, his protections and provision lasted about 13 months.

The amazing coincidence? Our 2nd *sign of Jonah* will also appear on this exact day, known to the world as April/8/2024 when yet another massive, continent-spanning eclipse is projected to appear over the USA. As stated earlier, I believe this to be a sign to those few who are left, that it is all finished.

5-Months of Torment and Strong Delusions before death!

Fun Facts: "...*because of this will God will send to them a strong delusion....*" Now, in Greek, this was interesting to find.

First, let's deal with the phrase "strong delusion." I have never believed anything in the Christian commentaries (NT) to have originated from the Greek language. And if any has, surely none of it was anything spoken by Yehshua. But for now, we will stick with the Greek because you will also see how the ancient Hebrew and Aramaic also agree.

(Strong delusion) – The Greek word used is – (**energia**). Which pretty much in all western languages carries that same spelling and meaning from the Greek = ENERGY! *Meaning* – A direct operation of energy. Now, remember, this is about a destructive deluding force.

(Strong delusion) – Hebrew word was – (**Toqef**) - (תֹּקֶף). *Which literally means* – Strong-Power or Energy! This word is used quite a bit in Daniel in regard to Babylon's overwhelming power and might.

Believe what you wish, but these prophecies all continue to point to something more specific than alien invasions or the United Nations world armies using manmade Tesla ray guns and mind control weapons. Not that we should fully rule that out as being the tools used by Yehovah to mete out said wide-scale punishment, but as I already posited regarding the role of the *Shayatim*, it appears to something more. Mainly because the prophecies clearly tell us that "ALL" of them will be overcome by it. So how could it be from them? Only the Sealed will not be affected at all.

Either way, this "Strong delusion" is clearly being described as an "Energetic power" used by Yehovah to create mass chaos which creates the same situation as we saw happen with the ancient giants.

Nothing changes. If Yehovah unleashed those *Shayatim-Jinn* before, likely it will happen again. The masses wanted to revel and bathe themselves in the blood of innocents. Back then, and since then, unabated. So surely, they will be made to bathe themselves in the blood of their own kind until none remain of them. Exactly as the Isaiah 13,14,15 & 16 prophecies depict for Moab/USA! And all eyes will watch via the mass media and see her smoke rising up!

"God" - "*...because of this will **God** will send to them a strong delusion....*" Also interesting, is how in other areas of these Thessalonian texts they use *another* Greek word which people have seemed to misunderstand as being the same reference to "The Prime Creator Source – AHEEYEH", but it is not.

Simply, in other sections of the Thessalonian text, and as I suspect the rest of the Christian NT, they actually and *correctly* seem to be differentiating between the *"mighty one – Elohim - Yehovah"* who is understood in the Hebrew Tanak as being the one who has control over this currently usurped, Satanic madhouse; versus the Prime Eternal Creator source, ***Aheeyeh*** who controls all. This is something I have not found in all of the Hebrew texts and or their translations.

"*...because of this will **God** will send to them a strong delusion....*"

Example: In much of the other Thessalonian texts when they were referring to this other entity as being a *direct influence*, they use the Greek word (**Kyrios**) which definitely appears to have the literal meaning of (Overlord/controller). With even the words more expanded meaning eluding to a more <u>localized control</u>. Which does, of course, concur exactly with how the world should have always seen the Elohim entity of *Yehovah* throughout the Hebrew texts, but were deliberately steered away from seeing.

Unlike the Greek word **Kyrios**, *and* as seen in some of the texts prior to this previous 2nd Thes 2:10 texts, we see the Greek word (**Theos**) being used here for "God" - "…*because of this will* **God** *will send…*." And if it isn't amazing enough that in such a deeply corrupted set of texts as the Christian new testament exists such an obvious example of truth as we see here with this differentiation of deity types and identities, that example is deepened by the literal meaning of (Theos) – *Meaning*, (Supreme Divinity) and more so, enfolding even the greater understanding in that Greek word as to mean - (of spontaneous existence!)

Theos – A supreme entity of spontaneous existence! Can only be referring to the Prime Eternal Creator of whose name means the same – AHEEYEH! *Meaning*, to exist and exist, forever. **FROM** forever to everlasting!

So, it would appear there are more things useful to us even among the heavily corrupted texts of the Christian NT than I previously gave credit for.

With the Sign of Jonah it Began, and Appears it will End:

It appears it will all end in the same way as we watched and received the prophesied warning on August/21st/2017. This was our warning to BE READY to begin counting off this 7-year Shmitah – (Not from the Roman date) but based on our calendar date of Asher-8.

Meaning, since we sighted the ¼ lighted moon phase on Neftali-1 last year in 2018 with great accuracy, which means on that day/night that same moon was also depicting a ¾ DARK side moon phase, which was the side of the moon that we were truly looking for inside of this new (Dark side) 7-year Shmitah cycle. [See Creator's Calendar 2019]

Which also means that last year's moon cycle proved not only the accurate timing of that year's Renewal-Memorial Day, but it also proved that a new 7-year Shmitah cycle began to count down. The FIRST sign of Jonah warned us, not only of what was coming but also to begin the count so that we have a good idea when it's coming, and for the expectation of protections and provisions through it all.

It is quite amazing that we will get another "sign of Jonah"- (eclipse over the USA) on April/8/2024, which as previously cited is our calendar day of NEFTALI-27th. And, as also previously stated, this is very significant because this is the sign of our "salvation", with Neftali being ruled under the sign known as the LAMB and the Shepherds' staff. I now believe that this *second sign of Jonah* will signify to those remaining that the Ark has made landfall, arrived safely and that all hostilities have ceased. The final eclipse will be our sign of the end of destructions and to our salvation and renewal.

This timing, from the beginning of the most horrific destructions upon the world which appears to take place over the span of one years' time, with its epicenter in the USA, and appears to begin

AFTER our 1st Renewal Memorial in 2022 – This Creator's calendar date coincides with the Roman date of (March/9/2022).

This 2022 date will be 3-Years from this past Renewal-Memorial Day in 2019 which coincided with the Roman date of (3/13/2019). As stated, this should begin the prophesied ONE YEAR *PLUS* of grand destructions as outlined by the Noah event date sequence, and as given in one of the Seven Warnings in this book. Most intriguing is that once again this END of destruction *Sign* that will come in 2024, occurs in nearly the identical span of time and pattern as it was in the days of Noah and proven out on the corrected Creator's calendar.

As Noah's protection and provisions lasted a bit over 1-year, so do these final events by ending almost 30-days after our 2024 Renewal Memorial.

What some may notice is that from the earlier, 2015 Jonah warnings (Ref Appendix-A; pg-50), where it depicts this time of *utter* chaos and destruction occurring over a span of about 1-year only, appears to be the culmination of that prophesied 3.5 years of apocalyptic destruction. *"…But if those days had not been shortened…"* Evidently, this overall timing as I am depicting here and in the next moon cycle picture <u>will be shortened</u> by just a bit.

Another point to consider is, that even though the open destructions might be quelled by then, that does not mean the aftermath of it won't linger profoundly. With such profound destruction as we witness in the prophetic Isaiah 13 -16 chapters, there will be no support mechanisms left for those surviving by the sweat of their brow to glean from. Their own crops and stored provisions will be made sufficient to last them through the rest of that 6th year to the coming Sabbatical year just as Noah's stock lasted them.

IN FAITH they will have to walk the path of the Everlasting Agreement, and by faith and obedience, their "oil" will be renewed as required, just as it was with the widowed woman who cried to

Elisha the prophet. Then, after this and by the 7th year their total provision will come. Yes, I believe there is enough prophetic proof showing that the Eternal One and His Legions will cause our 6th-year provisions to flourish and last. However, I also believe we have to take into consideration other prophetic events that must have space and time to play out within all of this. If we refer to the revised Shmitah moon phase picture, *below,* that I used in my Creator's Calendar guide book, it may be easier to discern how all this timing should work.

As I stated in the new calendar book, and as depicted in moon-picture #2 above, and as clearly proven by the 50/50% dark & light moon phase we all witnessed on the 2019 *Intercalary* night, we are in the SECOND year of the 7-year Shmitah cycle.

The moon cycles show the aforementioned 3.5 years from year-1 to the mid-point based on THIS calendar system, and from there it is 3.5 years to the end. **Simply stated** – From March/9/2022 we should see that 1-year of *Super-Judgment* to the next Renewal Memorial Day on March/8/2023, and possibly even a bit longer.

This now allows for those inside the Everlasting Agreement, and via the many prophecies on this point to receive favorable protections and provision, *miraculously* provided. I also do not believe it to be a stretch to say that from that time in 2022, that we may even be called and moved into His Greater Exodus. To me, this makes great sense because the prophesied destructions that are coming are so intense, happen so quickly, and so widespread that keeping His people moving into safer zones would most likely be the easiest way to keep them safe.

Whether we are moved or planted somewhere safe, many will be growing food while in that 6th year while being protected from annihilation. However, understand this, this is a point that so many have not understood correctly, and it will affect them while inside these calamities if not understood correctly.

As I have long taught through my Exodus 16 teaching, the provision of the Mannah on the 6th day – (a shadow of the 6th year), was NOT a double portion dropped by the Malakim of the Father and collected by the people on that 6th day in order to cover two days of food as alleged and twisted by the fraudulent scribes and most modern rabbis. No! The original instruction to Moshe was to have them collect a certain measure for the needs of their family for EACH DAY and let *Me* TEST them to see if they will obey and have total FAITH in *Me,* **on the Sabbath 7th day**. Which of course many did not, and will not, soon again. The original giving of the Sabbath was also a shadow of the future events. The Eternal One will enhance and aid the production of our food by our hands in that 6th years and until we come into His Sabbatical, 7th year. Then *He* will provide it all to those who have believed.

Correlations to Noah

If we look at the month of Rueben page in our calendar you will notice that all of Noah's journey ended on Fridays - on the 6th day. Those days being the 10th – 17th and 24th days. These all fall on the SIXTH day of the week. The 10 and 17th days being seven days apart are the days that Noah sent out the Raven and the Dove. On that 24th day of Rueben is when Noah sent that Dove out again, but it never returned. This is when we are told the waters were abating quickly.

Gen 8:6 *"And it came to pass <u>at the end of 40-days</u>, Noah opened the window of the ark which he had made:"* **[Reuben 10 – Day BEFORE the Sabbath!]**

[7] *"And <u>he sent out a raven</u> which went out and all around until the waters were dried up from off the earth;* [8] *<u>he also sent out a dove</u> to see if the waters were abated from off the face of the ground;* [9] *but the dove found no rest for the sole of her foot, and she returned to him into the ark, for the waters remained on the face of the whole earth: He took her and pulled her into the ark –* **[This all took place in one day on Reuben 10]** [10] *<u>and Noah remained another seven days</u>.-* **[7 days after Reuben-10 = Reuben 17 = day before the Sabbath again – Noah re-launches Dove.]**

[11] *Again, he sent out the dove from the ark;* **[On Reuben 17 BEFORE Sabbath]** - *<u>And the dove came into him in the evening</u>;* **[on the 17th]** *<u>and in her mouth was an olive leaf</u>: So, <u>Noah knew</u> that the waters were receding from off the earth".* [Noah received his 2nd sign and knew they were finally safe]

Gen 8:12 *"And he stayed yet <u>another 7-days</u>;* **[Reuben 24 and BEFORE yet another Sabbath day]** *- and sent forth the dove; which returned not again unto him any more."*

NOTE: Realize, that the ark and the other animals are still closed up and in hibernation at this time.

Also realize, that by this time Noah and the Ark were still inside that 600th Year. "<u>6" being the key in all this so far as we correlate it to the 6th Shmitah year and events coming</u>. These things, his protections through the flood in the 600th year, and his final protections coming on these three 6th-day event patterns show the continuing saga. YES, they were obviously protected inside the ark and possibly even had their food stores expanded as needed, but I think we see in the month of Rueben with all of the events happening on the 6th day – as it will be in the 6th Shmitah year – It was AT THAT TIME, near the end of that year when Noah received his second sign – *the dove and branch on the 17th-day.*

Noah's second sign told him they were safe, and would soon be fully provisioned (Outside of the Ark).

Meaning, it was obviously **the usual protections and provisions** for them **while inside the ark**, *but,* the real abundant provisions for both them and the animals (which they had no hand in) did not come until AFTER the end, *and not before everything on the ground began growing abundantly for them*.

Gen 8:13 *"And it came to pass in the 601st-year, in the 1st month, on the 1st-day of the month, the waters were dried up from off the earth: and Noah removed the covering of the ark, and looked, and, saw that the face of the ground was dry.* [This falls directly on the next year's 1st Renewal Memorial Day!]

Gen 8:14 *"And in the 2nd-month, on the 27th day of the month, was the earth fully dried."*

Gen 8:15 *"And God spoke to Noah, saying, 16 'Go from the ark, you, and your wife, and sons, and sons' wives and 17 bring out with you every living soul with you of all flesh, of fowl, and of cattle, and of every creeping thing that creeps upon the earth; that they may breed abundantly in the earth, and be fruitful, and multiply upon the earth. 18 And Noah went out, and his sons, and his wife, and his sons' wives with him: 19 "Every beast, every creeping thing, and every fowl, and all that creeps upon the earth, after their kinds, went out from the ark."*

They did NOT leave the Ark's protections and provisions until the start of that 7th Sabbatical year. And not until the spring where the ground was fully ready to flourish by the hand of the Eternal One. I have no doubt in my mind that while still inside the ark for those last days before the 1st Renewal Memorial of that 601st Sabbatical year, that the Eternal One hyper-accelerated the edible and medicinal fauna and flora so that when they emerged, they were fully provisioned thereafter.

Try connecting our future events back to Noah like this; We were told we would get the Sign of Jonah, but he never said how many times we would see that sign. Thus, in my mind, I am seeing that second sign of Jonah exactly in the same way that Noah saw the return of the final dove w/branch. THAT WAS A SIGN to Noah that all hostilities have ended. Get it?

Noah's FIRST SIGN was the HARD rain; and his second, FINAL SIGN was the dove and branch.

So, if hostilities begin, or at least become exponentially worse starting in 2022 for a year or so, and into 2023 – the 6th year, then, <u>*as it was in the days of Noah*</u>, it should "abate" again, possibly in that same 10th month of that 6th year, and of course, on the 6th day!

However, this would still be prior to our full-on provisions beginning anew in the Sabbatical year. Like Noah, wherever we are, we will still have to remain inside that *ark* with sleeping animals until we get past the 7th years 1st Renewal Memorial on Neftali-1 and into that new years', 2nd month again =Yissachar on the 27th-day when our completed provisions arrive.

We have seen our first sign, pray that when this comes, we will all see the second sign.

The End of Captivity in New Egypt

Is 2019 the end of the prophesied 400 years?

From the Apocalypse of Abraham

Chapter 32

1. "Therefore, hear Abraham, and see; *'Behold your seventh generation will go with you.* 2. *And they will go out into an <u>alien land</u>.* 3. *And they will enslave them and oppress them for one hour of the iniquitous age.* 4. *But of <u>the nation</u> whom they will be enslaved, I am the judge.'* And the Lord said this too; 'Do you hear, Abraham, what I told you? What your lineage will encounter **<u>in the last days</u>**?'

6. Abraham, having heard, accepted the words of the Eternal One in his heart.

Interestingly, the apocryphal book titled, *The Apocalypse of Abrahim*, of which appears to be enough direct and proven ancient correlations to the *Tanak*, the *Midrash*, *Jubilees*, the *Targum*, *Baruch* and by Jewish scholar *Rabbi Eliezer* to allow us to consider the accounts in it to have been recited from more ancient texts, and in some cases do provide a bit more detail over the *authorized* text.

I have long believed that the lineages of the tribes of Abrahim and sons were moved to a land far off, and one that they and all of their previous generations never knew existed. *Obviously, this cannot be said about their stay in Egypt or later, Assyria*. Jeremiah and other prophets go a long way to give us very detailed directional data and even topographical data as signs to those who pay attention. I have also long believed that most of those lineages, <u>all twelve</u>, were moved to the USA. And I am not nearly alone in that belief, and the evidence of it abounds if one wishes to chase it.

Recently, there are those out there who also believe that the end-time events are directly upon us. Believing and teaching that we, the USA, have traversed the allotted time of <u>400-years</u> from the Jamestown colony beginnings of 1619. Add <u>400 years</u> to 1619 and we arrive at 2019! Admittedly, I am finding that somewhat compelling given all else that I know concerning the prophecies of the tribes being relocated and finally released from captivity from Greater Egypt in the last days via the 2nd and Greater Exodus to come.

I find it equally interesting because much of what they are concluding about this 400 year period does line up within our corrected Creator's calendar. They, however, are all using the Jewish and other corrupted calendar systems, while at the same time seeking and speaking about this great "harvest" to come.

Interesting word *Harvest* in the Hebrew culture. Anyone who is acquainted with my other books knows that I have relied heavily on the prophet Yehshua's parables of the wheat & tares which revolve around the harvest of souls.

So, we have a 400 year period of enslavement in some far off and unknown land prophesied by Abrahim to conclude in the End-days; Then we have an actual 400 year period of sojourning in Egypt which later turned into indentured servitude before being released in that first exodus;

Then we have the Hebrew word:

[Reaping / Harvest – קציר – Katzeer] And, if we add up all of the numerical values of the letters therein, the sum is 400!

Then we have the Hebrew letter (Tav), which is the 22nd letter of the Hebrew alphabet, it is also <u>the last</u> and <u>final</u> letter in the alphabet.

Additionally, (Tav) also carries with it the numerical value <u>of 400</u> and the deeper meaning of a *Mark* or *Sign!* Thus, 400 is also a Mark/Sign.

So, at the very least this 400 number is sure making the rounds these days and seeming to connect to all manner of prophecy.

Of course, literally, everyone who ever read these *Apocalypse of Abrahim* texts instantly identifies them with the 1st Egyptian captivity and subsequent Exodus. The problem with that is, that the texts clearly divulge when the prophetic timeframe will be – IN THE LAST DAYS! The importance of understanding that these texts are connected prophetically to the rest cannot be overstated.

Jer 16:13 *"And I have cast you from off this land, <u>and to a land that you have not known, not you or your fathers</u>! And you will serve their other gods by day and by night, where I do not give to you mercy."*

There are ample prophetic texts which clearly depict this same sentiment. That they would be moved to totally new places and redeemed at a later time – In the acceptable YEAR!

Isa 61:1 *"The Spirit of the mighty one Yehovah is on me, because Yehovah has anointed me to cheerfully announce, to sow and to bind up the broken-hearted, to proclaim freedom to captives, and opening prisons to the bound ones; 2 <u>to proclaim the acceptable year of the Eternal One</u>, and <u>the day of vengeance</u> of Yehovah; to comfort all who mourn;"*

If memory serves me, I believe I recall Yeshua reading these exact words in the Yeshiva. I always found that quite interesting, that Yeshua read those verses. Especially since I have always known that he was an Essene, which also meant that he knew and followed the 1st law of the *Everlasting Agreement*. And *that* is exactly the Agreement that Isaiah was made to prophesy about, which means that these Isiah 61 texts must also be speaking to the Everlasting Agreement as well. Has to be, because Isaiah is one of the prophets "of" the Everlasting Agreement. Which then, by default is further proof that the great prophet Yehshua was also proclaiming the 1st law of the Everlasting Agreement as he spoke these same words.

Full circle. From the mouth of the prophet to the mouth of the Essene Grand Master who is most likely the very *Elect one* spoken of by Enoch who will cause the entire world to revert back to the way of the Garden, via the Eternal Creators, Everlasting Agreement!

So, it appears this *Acceptable Year* won't be at the end of, or LAST year of the Shmitah cycle, but during the 7-year cycle - <u>to proclaim the</u> acceptable year of the Eternal One, and <u>the day of vengeance of Yehovah</u>..."

Again, this would also appear to line up with the building disruptions to utter destructions by Yehovah if this, in fact, began in 2019. At which point, the 400-year *final* release from captivity via the prophecy of Abrahim and other prophets will come in that Sabbatical year as prescribed earlier.

Could it be that we are seeing yet another portion of this expanding puzzle of the end times events, and timing?

- 400 years being used as a sign;
- The letter Tav = 400 as a sign;
- Tav as the final, ending letter;
- Tav meaning Mark or Sign;
- Tav the 22nd letter – 22 & 2022;
- The Reaping - קציר = 400 as a sign;

Apoc of Abram 30: 58. *"See, Abrahim, what you have seen, and hear what you have heard, and understand all that you have come to know. Go to your heritage, and behold, I am with you forever."*

59. 'But while He was still speaking to me, I found myself once again upon the earth, and I said, "0 Eternal One! I am no longer in the glory which is on high, and there is one matter which my soul longed to know and understand which has not been revealed to me.

60. And He said to me, "What your heart desired I will tell you because you have sought to see <u>the ten plagues</u> which I have prepared for the godless <u>nations</u>, and which have been <u>pre-determined at the **passing-over**</u> of the <u>twelfth hour of the age</u> of the earth. Hear therefore what I divulge, and so will it come to pass. **[He never changes!]**

1. The first is the distressing pain of sickness; - **[Shayatim-Jinn?]**
2. The second, the burning of many cities;
3. The third, the destruction and pestilence of animals;
4. The fourth, hunger of the whole world and its people;
5. The fifth, <u>destruction by its rulers</u>, by earthquake and the sword; **[War]**
6. The sixth, the multiplication of hail and snow; **[Due to war]**
7. The seventh, wild bests will be their grave;
8. The eighth, hunger and pestilence will alternate with destruction; **[War]**
9. The ninth, punishment by the sword and flight in distress; **[War or Jinn]**
10. The tenth, thunder <u>and voices</u> and destructive earthquake. **[Jinn]**

[Who was the first Death Angel? The Jinn!]

Beginning with 30:60; "...see <u>the ten plagues</u> which I have prepared for the godless <u>nations</u>...;

Again, without paying attention most will read these and believe them to be Abrahim receiving the foreknowledge of the first Egyptian slavery and plagues, but that would be incorrect. Notice it clearly says [nations?] And all things being equal, one cannot really describe Egypt as a "godless" nation. They were blessed beyond all others for a long time, and even more so when the Hebrew's arrived. So, this is clearly prophetic of the end times as the Abrahimic texts previous to these depicted.

"...which have been <u>pre-determined at the passing-over</u> of the <u>twelfth hour of the age</u>..." There are 12 ages of 2600 years each as represented

by the 12 tribes as depicted in the original version of the Creator's calendar. [See Asher:2019, Creator's Calendar]. **Are we there yet?**
31: 61. *And <u>then I</u> [Aheeyeh] <u>will sound the trumpet</u> out of the air, and will send <u>My Elect One</u>, having in him all my power in one measure, and <u>he will summon my despised people from all nations</u>, and fire will fall upon those who have insulted them and who have ruled over them <u>in this age</u>. And I will give those who have covered me with mockery to the scorn <u>of the coming age</u>, they are prepared to be food for the fires of Hades, and perpetual flight through the air in the underworld, then they will see the righteousness of the Creator, and those whom I now honor. And they will be ashamed, <u>for I had hoped that they would</u> **Return** <u>to me in repentance</u>, rather than loving strange gods, but they forsook the Mighty Eternal One and went the way that they willed to go.*

Well, if I didn't show the existence and position of the Elect one via the Enochian texts enough throughout my body of work, here he is spoken of again in a totally unrelated codex. "*….having in him all my power in one measure, and <u>he will summon my despised people from all nations</u>…*" And having the ability to judge everyone else by fire and all manner of other powers that the Eternal Creator Aheeyeh has. I know that I have heard the exact claims about Yehshua from Christians my entire life. So, this may be yet another circumstantial proof, and one of many that he is in fact, the Elect one.

"*…. and <u>he will summon my despised people from all nations</u>…*" And here we have a clear reference to the coming, 2nd and Greater Exodus! Just as I have shown many times before using other prophetic texts, that the Elect one will head up the Greater Exodus. [See Asher:2012, Greater Exodus]

"*….<u>for I had hoped that they would Return to me in repentance</u>…;*"
There it is again! But if you do not know that the 1st law of the *Everlasting Agreement* exists, believing the lie that the 2nd law of Sinai is the only law that exists, then you would never see this part

for what it is. And there are so many just like it throughout the Torah, prophets and historical writings which continue to go unnoticed. As I always ask: Why would the Eternal One, through His many prophets continually ASK us to RETURN-TESHUVAH, if we as souls didn't LEAVE Him and His path behind? Why would He ask us to Return if there is nothing to Return to? Most importantly, why would He ask us to Return if there was no way for us to do it?

All more evidence of the same once you know what to look for.

It is rather compelling when we add it all into that which I have already presented herein regarding Noah's calamities and our end of days events.

The Apocalypse of Abraham belongs to a body of Abrahamic literature from the mid-first century. It is believed by scholars that the book was written in Hebrew and essentially Jewish with features that suggest an Essene origin. From the Essenes, it was believed passed to the Ebionites, and later, in some form found its way into Gnostic circles and added to.

Exodus 16: The Quail and the Mannah

The following teaching is to provide the corrected framework regarding the Eternal's basic daily provisions for us, versus His greatly expanded provisions which we receive only by obedience and faith that He will follow through. This crucial understanding has been greatly twisted by the priests and scribal editors.

Ex - 16:1 "And they took their journey from Elim, and all the congregation of the children of Jacob came to the wilderness of Sin, which is between Elim and Sinai, on the 15th day of the 2nd month after their departing out of the land of Egypt."

Verse 16:1 was added by the final redactors from the [Stations list -aka - Book of Numbers].

All LIGHT GRAY texts herein were texts that were added much later, between 850 - 500BCE by the **Priestly redactor source** – believed in Judaic tradition to have been the Levite Priest-Scribe Ezra. This is not to say that *all* Priestly texts are totally false. However, most were added or augmented in the entire Tanak to uphold their later, Babylonian Talmudic agenda. As you will also see herein, their texts are not really needed to tell the whole story. As well, they make many parts appear redundant and leave most English readers with more questions than answers.

The "**Oldest Source**" texts are from the oldest source scrolls which the redactors had in Babylon. These have been dated to be from around 1250, BC, and of course, that puts them extremely close to Moshe who actually wrote these words. All else was cut & pasted during the time of Ezra and after from many source texts which spanned many years, as well as totally unrelated texts. In some cases with missing data from the oldest scrolls, there is no doubt why later scroll sources had to be tapped to fill in those sections for context. However, as I have long proven, this is not the only reason why those later source texts and even data from no source texts were added by those contemporary scribes.

2 And the whole congregation of the children of Jacob murmured against Moses and Aaron in the wilderness: 3 And the children of Jacob said to them, it would have been better if the Eternal One had killed us in the land of Egypt, <u>when we sat cooking meats</u>, and when we ate bread to the full; for you have brought us forth into this wilderness, to kill this whole assembly with hunger.

Oldest Source: *4 The Eternal One said to Moses, 'Behold, I will rain bread from heaven for you; and the people will go out and gather a certain amount <u>every day</u>, <u>that I may test them</u>, whether they will walk in my Instruction, or not. 5 And, <u>on the sixth day,</u> <u>they will use</u> what they collect, <u>and it will be twice as much as they gathered</u>.* [This is proof of a 7th day Sabbath miracle since all is commanded to be used up in that sixth day.]

6 And Moses and Aaron said to all the children of Jacob: 'at evening, then you will know that the Eternal One has brought you out from the land of Egypt: 7 'And in the morning, you will see the power of the Eternal One; for he hears your murmurings against Him: and who are we, that you murmur against us?

8 And Moses said, 'this will be when the Eternal One <u>will give you in the evening flesh to eat</u>, and in the morning bread to the full; for the Eternal One hears your murmurings which you murmur against him: And who are we? Your murmurings are not against us, but against Him.'

You, do not have to be a scholar to see how the new context of verses 6-8 is suddenly popped in here?

First off, the Eternal One will in no way give anyone meat to eat at any time, nor will His legions, this precept can be proven all the way back to Genesis-1 and also via Noah. That the Eternal Creator's character is set, never changing and thus, is the proof we always use to identify and nullify all such added texts and later teachings.

The Eternal One <u>will not change</u> and go against His absolute command of the Everlasting Agreement.

However, if you are attempting to install the proof that He *allows* and even *commands* such a thing in order to gain the authority, then yes, this is exactly what you might add and certainly, you will always add these texts into the places where the highest Torah authority is speaking. *Like Moshe.*

Now, a bit off-topic for the calendar, but a point I always love to point out - WHY exactly are they murmuring for MEAT? If memory serves, were we not previously told in Exodus 12, *just weeks prior to this account in 16,* that they RUINED Egypt and left with tens of thousands of head of cattle of all types? Wasn't it specifically Pharaoh who told Moshe to get out and take the cattle with you? Actually, the question you should all be asking is; *'HOW did Moshe even hear their incessant complaining over the cry of ALL that cattle?'* One of many proofs from my **Land of Meat & Honey** book depicting – THAT THE LAW PROVIDED JUST PRIOR TO LEAVING EGYPT FORBID THE MURDER AND CONSUMPTION OF THE ANIMALS! You don't murmur for beef, lamb or birds when it's all standing right there next to you UNLESS someone already told you they were forbidden fruit!

9 "And Moses said to Aaron; 'say to all the congregation of the children of Jacob, come near before the Eternal One: for he has heard your murmurings.' 10 And it came to pass, as Aaron spoke to the whole congregation of the children of Jacob, that they looked toward the wilderness, and, behold, the glory of the Eternal One appeared in the cloud."

I would also like to point out something else somewhat unrelated here. You will continue to notice that the Priestly texts always install Aaron throughout their texts into a position as an equal authority to Moshe. This was NEVER so, and Moshe was the ONLY one given ANY authority at all. This has been cleverly salted throughout the texts in order to give their false Levitical priesthood the air of ultimate authority. Just because the Messenger of the Eternal One told you to take the guy standing nearby with you because he could speak more eloquently than you, DOES NOT mean that the great authority given you as Lawgiver is diminished by 50%.

11 "And the Angel of the Eternal One spoke to Moses, saying; 12 'I have heard the murmurings of the children of Jacob: speak to them, saying, <u>At evening you will eat flesh</u>, and in the morning you will be filled with bread; and you will know that I am the Eternal One, your God.' 13 And it came to pass, that at evening the quails came up, and covered the camp: and in the morning the dew lay round about the host."

Ok, hold on right here, because I know everyone is going straight to Numbers for this one. Most of you know that I don't believe Numbers to be anywhere near original Torah, most of which is re-scribed stories taken directly out of early original Torah of Exodus like we will see here with additions from what is known as – The Stations list. However, I have never ruled out that this entire story could be true, and that the "angel" in the scene was the taskmaster Yehovah. We know that he is the one who delivers all judgment, and if we look at it this way, this is certainly judgment. Yes, the birds were sent there, but those who CHOSE and CONSENTED to kill and eat them made their choice and received the punishment – Death! How is that any different from the majority of people in the world during the end-days ignoring the warnings and even openly deriding the Two Witnesses, and then tacitly consenting to their murders? It's always the same choice, and because HE does NOT change, then His legions are set to deliver the same result.

Num 11:31-34 *"Then, the Messenger of the Eternal One sent a wind, driving little birds from the sea so that they came down on the tents, and all around the tent perimeter, and outward about a day's journey on this side and on that, in masses about two cubits high over the face of the earth. 32 And all that day and all night and the day after, many people were collecting the birds; the smallest amount which anyone got was <u>ten omers</u>. And they stacked them out all around the tents. 33 But while the meat was still between their teeth, and before it was tasted, the wrath of Yehovah moved against the people and he sent a great outburst of disease on them. 34 So that place was named Kibroth-hattaavah; because there they put in the earth the bodies of the people who had given way to their desires."*

".... But while the meat was <u>still between their teeth</u>, and <u>before it was tasted</u>, the wrath of Yehovah moved against the people...."

Well, there it is! They CHOSE! They CONSENTED to ignore the warning of the ONE Messenger at that time, and the example was made. Does anyone truly believe that if the majority of the people witnessed this happen to friends and loved ones, that they later played fast and loose with their lives and that of their children's lives by murdering even more animals for sacrifice and eating that meat? Ignore the Witness of the Father at your peril and that of your own soul's eternal separation.

Additionally, unlike most traditional teachings that say, '*as soon as it touched their lips they died on the spot*,' the Hebrew does not uphold that idea and neither does this English translation. The only other issue I take with these texts and virtually the entire Tanak for that matter is that all translations of these texts have been taught to all generations as to always show the Yehovah entity as being the Eternal Creator, Himself, <u>which is NOT true</u>. And, as I have taught for nearly a lifetime now, this practice and subsequent belief have caused all manner of misunderstanding and even disdain for the Creator directly. Disdain for being a "god" of destruction and hate, etc. The total misunderstanding of who each entity is and what their position is within the *Sefirot*.

More importantly, the knowledge that original laws have always existed, and that the 2nd Law, *aka, Deuteronomy* as given later on Mt. Sinai after their rebellion of the 1st law of the Everlasting Agreement occurred, that THIS was when they were fully given over to that law. And of course, fully given over to the one who presides over this place and that 2nd law specifically – Yehovah. Yes, he is the one crushing it throughout the books, but only after people CHOSE and CONSENTED to break those 2nd laws. In the end, he is NOT the Eternal Creator.

Now you know not to fall into their trap of attributing the negative outcomes of people and animals to the Eternal Creator, directly. The overall point here which I started to point by showing the Numbers text, was to bring your attention to how the much later scribes, after leaving Babylonian captivity brought the Exodus 16 story of the quail forward. *"and they did eat manna until they came to the borders of the land of Canaan".* Which means the Eternal One's Messengers provided ONLY Mannah as their *clean* food source.

Cont:

14 And when the dew that lay evaporated, behold, upon the face of the wilderness there lay a small round thing, as small as frost on the ground. 15 And when the children of Jacob saw it, they said one to another, "mannah!": for they knew not what it was. And Moses said to them, this is the bread which the Eternal One has given you to eat. [Mah'nah is ancient Egyptian for – What is this?]

16 This is the thing which the Eternal One has commanded; 'Gather of it every man according to his eating, an omer for every man, according to the number of your persons; take some for every person in your tents.' 17 And the children of Jacob did so and gathered some more, and some less. 18

And when they measured it with an omer, he that gathered much [Gluttons] *had nothing left over, and he that gathered little had no lack; they gathered every man according to his eating.*

19 And Moses said, 'Let no man leave of it till the morning.'

20 but they hearkened not to Moses, and some of them kept some until the morning, and it bred worms, and rotted: and Moses was wroth with them."

Oldest Source: *21 "And they gathered it <u>every morning</u>, [of the 6 days] every man <u>according to his eating</u>: and when the sun waxed hot, it melted."*

Here we see yet again another reiteration of the same, but from the more ancient source scrolls which reads far more simply – 'To gather the ONE Omer for EACH person daily, for the SIX days!

22 "Then it happened, that on the sixth day <u>some gathered twice as much Mannah, two omers for one man: and all the Elders of the congregation came and told Moses</u>".

WAIT! Why did the elders come to Moshe with this grave concern if the law was such to do just that, as the rabbis have always taught it to be? By the context of the Priestly source text of verse 22, it has to be concerning their gathering of <u>twice as much on the 6th day</u>, right? However, all the rabbis say, *based on this chapter* that they were supposed to gather 2x more on Friday. Which you will see disproven herein later on. Thus far there has been no instruction [from the messenger of the Eternal] telling them to gather more on day 6th to cover the entire Sabbath days meals! YOU SEE? Their own Priestly source text gives them away. [*And all the elders came to Moshe...*] Yes, they came to Moshe to express concern at the fact that the people were taking more than originally commanded for **each** of the six days. This proves that the ACTUAL, original instruction was based on their having FAITH *to a miracle* on each and every Sabbath day.

Additionally, I also believe that the texts from both sources show how the Messengers of the Eternal One also "regulated" everyone's Mannah intake daily. As it is written, those gluttons who could not follow directions on all six days and took more than they really needed, had their Mannah jars depleted by just enough; and those who didn't feel the need to take the whole amount each day had their jars added to. These are miracles happening "in" the six-day period!

Only within the priestly texts did they write this scene in such a way as to *elude* to this DOUBLE portioning of Mannah as being a physical gathering of this double portion by their own hands, on day six. This depiction is quite clever, as it totally negates the elder texts which depict this as a miracle from the Eternal One Himself and His provision for their double portions. Very clever!

Their jars of *oil* or Mannah, in this case, were miraculously regulated during the week, and their lack of food stores on each 7th day was miraculously provided. Just as His people will be regulated through the 6th year and then fully provisioned through the 7th Sabbatical year to come.

DO YOU WANT YOUR PORTIONS BY FAITH IN THAT 7TH SABBATICAL YEAR TO COME? *I DO!*

23 "And he said to them – [the elders] *- 'this is what the Eternal One has said; 'Tomorrow is the rest of the holy Sabbath to the Eternal One: bake that which you will bake today, and boil what you will boil; and that which remains, keep until the morning."* Ahh… Leftovers! Again, as with the Widow woman's oil. She had a little left-over oil, but not enough. And the Eternal One, by her faith, added to her small portion daily.

24 "And they kept the leftover till morning, as Moses said: and it did not rot, nor was there any worms in it". – They kept some leftover from that which was not used up on Friday, which could in no way be enough for three more meals on the Sabbath day. Another obvious proof that their Mannah was miraculously added to as the day wore on.

25 "And Moses said, 'Eat that today; for today is a Sabbath to the Eternal One. Today you will not find it in the field. 26 Six days you will gather it, but on the seventh day there will be none."

Oldest Source: *27 "And it came to pass, that there went out some of the people on the seventh day to gather, and they found none."*

WHY? Didn't the Priest source texts just tell us that the double portions that THEY collected by their own hands would be enough for the Sabbath day, AND, that it would remain viable for that day so that everyone would have their daily bread? But now the oldest source texts, *which are very simple and plain to understand if you have not yet noticed,* are telling us that some people evidently did not have any Mannah in the house on the Sabbath after Fridays meals, so they went out looking for more on the Sabbath? What are we seeing here?

What you are seeing is more proof! Here is how this went down and will go down again in the coming Sabbatical year. They were clearly told to pick up ONLY enough Mannah EACH DAY, over SIX days, and that they would be PROVIDED their Mannah by the Eternal One on the Sabbath day. EMPTY POTS MADE FULL!

So, the reason we see this story explaining how some went out on the Sabbath morning to FIND Mannah, is because those were the people **who did not at all believe** in their hearts that they would be maintained. And thus, they were NOT maintained. So in the end, I guess they were correct! No Mannah came for *them*!

Is this also not unlike the story of the Virgins with their oil?

Song of Solomon 1:3 *"The passing scent is perfect, like oil, your name [Aheeyeh] is an ointment poured out <u>on the upright</u> <u>virgins</u> with love."*
[Asher literal translation]

This is ALL about miracles that cannot be explained away by any black-robed priest or scribe with a silly hat! It's about full-on, in your face miracles like a pillar of fire and clouds for shade and mega protections from all invaders, etc. This is about an empty refrigerator that refills nightly and somehow remains cold without electricity. This is about water that pumps up from a deep well without power to the pump! This is NOT about half-hearted events that may or may not be a miracle from some god or angel. When the Eternal One through His legions does it to you, you will NOT be confused about how it happened or who did it. Let all those Babylonian Shelanites spend their time toiling for supplies and sitting around debating how it did or did not happen, and or who may have done it.

Oldest source: *28 "And the Messenger of the Eternal One said to Moses; 'How long will you refuse to keep my instructions!" 29 "See! The Eternal One has given you the Sabbath!* **He provides** <u>*for you six days and the bread of another day!*</u> *Now! Every man will remain in his place! No man will go out of his dwelling on the seventh day! 30 So, the people remained in their dwellings on the seventh day."*

NOTE: First, I can tell you that the previous 16:28-30 texts are generally mistranslated, horrifically in most versions. Of course, they have been mistranslated, if not, nothing that came before or after them would uphold their false narrative which dilutes the *divine intervention* by such an obvious miracle, ongoing. *Secondly,* you will notice that I changed all of the horrifically misplaced punctuation. Poorly placed punctuation within all western language translations is nothing new, it is known to change the meanings of many texts. Here in these previous texts, it is now obvious to the reader that Moshe was the recipient of one upset Messenger of the Eternal One.

Another major point here that few understand correctly, and one that will have a direct effect on many people who believed they were covered by His presence when the balloon goes up someday; it is also a precept governed by the undeniable truth that the Eternal One NEVER CHANGES –

"…. *No man will go out of his dwelling on the seventh day!* [30] *So, the people remained in their dwellings on the seventh day…."*

What few understand, and that which the Babylonian Shelanites have always known and circumvented by any means to this day *is that this Sabbath day quarantine has NEVER been lifted*.

Which means, by obedience, this Sabbath day quarantine is yet another point of obedience within the fabric of His Everlasting Agreement. It is NOT negotiable! I have written about this in more detail in my Asher Codex.

Isa 26:20 *"Come, my people, go into your dwellings, and shut the doors, hide yourselves for a short time until the indignation passes over."* [21] *"Behold! Yehovah comes out of his place to punish the inhabitants of the earth for their iniquity! The earth will also disclose her blood, and will no more cover her slain."*

Do you see? This and other prophetic texts of the same line up with that *prohibition of leaving our dwellings* on the Sabbath day. Although the prohibition began as punishment for their original disobedience, it was also set in place by the One who knows and sees all as an ongoing *practice* for those who remain fully obedient to the details. If one recalls the Creator's calendar teachings, and also recalls the admonishment of Yehshua who stated that when the end days begin, that it would be better if it did not begin in the **winter** or on a **Sabbath day**. Well, by the corrected Creator's calendar, the 1335th day is at the beginning of winter, AND, <u>on a Sabbath day</u>! Thus, all the Yeshurim better be inside their homes on that day and every Sabbath day from this day to that one.

Cont:

> 16: 31 *"And the house of Jacob called the name of it Mannah: and it was like coriander seed, white; and the taste of it was like wafers made with honey. 32 And Moses said, 'This is the thing that the Eternal One commands; 'Fill an omer of it to be kept for your generations; that they may see the bread wherewith I have fed you in the wilderness when I brought you forth from the land of Egypt.'*
>
> *33 And Moses said to Aaron; 'Take a pot, and put an omer full of manna in it, and lay it up before the Eternal One, to be kept for all generations. 34 As the Eternal One commanded Moses, so Aaron laid it up before the Testimony, to be kept. 35 And the children of Jacob ate Mannah forty years, and until they came to a land inhabited....*
>
> Oldest Source: *".... And they did eat manna until they came to the borders of the land of Canaan."*
>
> ^{36} *"Now an omer is the tenth part of an ephah."*

Now, look at the way they ended this section from 33 to 36. These are the areas that should alert you to the priestly manipulations. And once again, the most ancient source text there is the only one required.

Are you beginning to see how to think about all this from the beginning to the final end as the calendar depicts it? Do you see how important it is to KNOW His true *character* and how it has all been woven into work for those who can SEE? Also making it obvious how they changed just enough to change the peoples' track. The track of the Everlasting Agreement which He lamented about through the prophet Isaiah – *that man has defiled that Everlasting Agreement and destroyed the earth*. They changed the calendars and caused *time* to become a cage for everyone.

From the much earlier source texts which they moved out of their original position which was in early Exodus. I have a large chapter on the two law versions in my Asher Codex.

Exo 31:12 *And the Jehovah spoke to Moses, saying;*
13 *"You speak to the sons of Sons of Jacob, saying, you will keep the sabbaths; for it is <u>a sign</u> between the Eternal and you for your generations, and to know that I am Jehovah your sanctifier. 14 And you will keep the Sabbath, for it is holy for you; the profaners of it will die; for everyone doing work in it, that soul will be cut off from the midst of his people."*

Exo 31:15 *"Work may be done six days, and on the seventh day is a sabbath of rest, holy to the Eternal; everyone doing work on the Sabbath day will die.*

Exo 31:16 *And the sons of Sons of Jacob will observe the Sabbath, to do the Sabbath for their generations <u>as a never-ending compact</u>.*

Exo 31:17 *It is a <u>sign forever between the Eternal One and the Sons of Jacob</u>; for in six days the Eternal One made the heavens and the earth, and on the seventh day He rested and was refreshed."*

It is a SIGN (The *Tav-400*-A Compact)

KNOWING who He is, then one will never have the most important tool we can have in identifying all the false narrative traditions.

NOW do we see why knowing the Creators calendar is so utterly important? And to know it to the point where you will NOT require any written material in your possession to keep it!

APPENDIX-A
The First Warning
8/15/2015

> **Gen 15:13** *"And He said to Abram; 'Understand, you must know that your seed will be an alien in a land, not theirs, and they will serve them. And they will afflict them four hundred years;*
>
> *¹⁴ and I will judge that nation whom they will serve, and afterward, they will come out with great substance."*

As these warnings come, it is understood that you should first ignore everything that is not seen as highlighted. For the original document, I left all the rest in between un-highlighted so the reader would have the total context if they need it, but try it first with only reading the highlighted sections. Also, all the highlighted prophetic sections should be understood as relating to our modern time, today and the near future. The following all came spread over four consecutive Sabbaths beginning in August of 2015.

I would also like to point out that I have made it my lifelong practice to refrain from any prophecy or the projections thereof that are outside of the single most provable prophecy of the Greater Exodus. I have refrained because there are countless others who try and fail, and truthfully my thinking has always been, *it will come when it does*. Adding to that, the Creator's calendar in its *corrected* form has been long lost to us until recently, and all prophecy depends on having and applying that calendar.

This is the first time I have been provided what appears to be a specific timeframe which obviously began in August of 2015, and doing so with extreme reluctance.

First Shabat: This portion seemed to be marking the Nation, the people, and destruction zones -

Isa 1:1 *"The vision of Isaiah the son of Amos, which he saw concerning Judah and Jerusalem in the days of Uzziah, Jotham, Ahaz and Hezekiah, kings of Judah. 2 Hear, O heavens, and listen O earth! For AHYH has spoken: I have nursed and brought up sons, but they have rebelled against Me, 3 the ox knows his owner, and the ass his master, but Jacob does not know; My people have no understanding. 4 Woe, sinful nation, a people heavy with iniquity, a seed of evildoers, sons who corrupt! They have forsaken AHYH; they have scorned the Holy One of Jacob. They are estranged, backward. 5 Why will you remain stricken? Will you continue the revolt? The whole head is sick, and the whole heart is weak. 6 From the sole of the foot to the head there is no soundness in it; only a wound, a cut, and a fresh bruise; they have not been closed, **nor bandaged**; nor softened with oil. [See Hoshea 6:1 below] 7 Your land is a desolation; your cities burned with fire. Foreigners devour your land before you; and behold, ruin, as overthrown by foreigners. 8 And the daughter of Zion is left like a booth in a vineyard, like a hut in a cucumber field, like a besieged city. 9 Had not AHYH of legions left a trace of a remnant, we would be as Sodom; we would be as Gomorrah.*

2nd Shabat: This one appeared to tell me who will be aided and why. Then frames the sin of murdering animals again, and that He will choose to allow the vexations *that they chose for others* to be put on them. <u>And again, stating that those remnants who are driven out will be the ones aided.</u>

Isa 66 - *"So says AHYH: Heaven is My throne, and earth the footstool of My feet. Where then is the house that you build for Me? And where then is the place of My rest? 2 My hand has made all these things, even all these things exist,* declares AHYH; *but I will look toward this one* [type]; *to the afflicted, to the contrite of spirit, those respectful of My instruction –* [Everlasting Agreement]. *3 He who kills an ox is as if he struck down a man; he who sacrifices a lamb is as if he broke a dog's neck; he who offers a sacrifice is as if it were swine's blood; he who supplicates with incense is as if he blessed an idol. Yes, they have chosen their way, and their soul delights in their abominations. 4 I also will allow their vexations; and I will bring their fears to them; because I called, and no one answered; I spoke, and they did not hear. But they did the evil in My eyes and chose that in which I hate. 5 Hear the Word of AHYH, all who revere His Word. Your brothers who hate you, who drive you out for My name's sake, have said, 'GOD is glorified'; **but AHYH will appear in your aid**, and they will be ashamed. 6 A sound of an uproar from the city! A call out from the temple! It is a call out of AHYH completing an action upon His enemies.* 7 Before she travailed, she brought forth; before pain came to her, she delivered a male child. 8 Who has heard a thing like this? Who has seen things like these? Will the earth be brought forth in one day? Will a nation be born in one step? For Zion travailed and also brought forth her sons. 9 Will I bring to the birth, and not cause to bring forth? Says AHYH. Surely, I cause birth, and hold back, says your God."

3rd Shabat: This one started out by plainly telling me to stop my incessant prayers for "them" as I tend to do. Then goes on again to frame the transgression against His Everlasting Agreement. Why would He stop me from praying for the majority of souls who retain no recall of their original and continual transgression, I thought. Granted, I tend to be a bit of a deal maker in our conversations, but as always, His answer was very simple and obvious – *"They do not even hear themselves when they speak, much less hear Me."* This was in the context of *the multitude,* who in all my years of trying to teach the Everlasting Agreement, *especially so and greatly amplified after I was made to write the first book on it,* they assume the position of the psychopath murderer in their arguments against it. As I stated in the LMH book, to argue against the Everlasting Agreement is to openly argue in favor of the murder of innocents who cannot defend themselves against us.

Thus, the Eternal One's point to me on this specifically goes to the simpler point; that it does NOT take access to our generational "soul-memories" to know that murdering innocents or anyone for our personal gain is wrong, and the opposite of "Life & Good."

Jer 7 - 16 "And you, do not pray for this people; do not lift up cry or prayer for them! Do not intercede with Me, for I will not hear you! 17 Do you not see what they are doing in the cities of Judah and in the streets of Jerusalem? 18 The sons gather wood, and the fathers kindle the fire, and the women knead dough, to make cakes to the queen of heaven, and to pour out drink offerings to other gods, that they may provoke Me. 19 Do they provoke Me, says AHYH? Is it not themselves, to the shame of their own faces? 20 So AHYH says this: Behold, my anger, and My fury will be poured out on this place, on man and on animal, and on the trees of the field, and on the fruit of the ground. And it will burn and will not be put out. 21 So says AHYH of legions, the God of Jacob: Add your burnt offerings to your sacrifices **and eat flesh.** 22 I did not speak to your fathers, nor command them in the day that I brought them out from the land of Egypt, concerning matters of burnt offerings and sacrifices. 23 But I commanded them this thing, saying, Obey My voice, and I will be your mighty one, and you will be My people. Also, walk in all the ways that I have commanded you, so that it may be well with you. 24 But they did not listen nor bow their *ear. But they walked in their own plans, in the stubbornness of their evil heart, and went backward and not forward. 25 Since the day that your fathers came out of the land of Egypt **until this day**, I have sent to you all My servants, the prophets, daily, rising up early and sending. 26 Yet they did not listen to Me nor bow their ear, but they stiffened their neck. **They do more evil than their fathers**.*

4th Shabat: Identifying the parties who left Him from the beginning to the present and identifying the transgression that caused it - Framing Mercy & wisdom over slaughtering. If you read my Greater Exodus book then you understand that Ephraim, Josef, and Judah are mostly here in the USA. And many researchers on the topic of the so-called "Lost tribes" have long believed the same. Of course, we remain scattered still, but for some end-days reason, most were moved here.

Hoshea 5:8-6:11 *"Blow a horn in Gibeah, a trumpet in Ramah. Cry aloud, Bet-aven; after you, O Benjamin. 5:9 Ephraim will be desolate in the day of correction! Among the tribes of Jacob, I have made known that which is confirmed. 10 The rulers of Judah were as movers of a border; I will allow wrath on them like water. 11 Ephraim is oppressed, crushed in judgment; because he was pleased he walked after the precept. 12 Therefore, I am as a moth to Ephraim, and to the house of Judah as rottenness. 6:1 Come and let us return to AHYH. For He has torn, and He will heal us. He has stricken, and He will **bandage** us up. 2 After **two days He will bring us to life. In the third day** He will raise us up, and we will live before Him.* - (See Isa 16:14 below) *3 Then **all will know, we who follow and know AHYH**. His going forth is established as the dawn. And He will come to us as the rain, as the latter and former rain to the earth. 4 O Ephraim, what will I do to you? O Judah, what will I do to you? For your* *goodness is like a morning cloud, and goes away like the early dew. 5 So, I have shaped them by the prophets; I have slain them by the Words of My mouth, <u>and your judgments have been as the light that goes forth</u>. 6 For I desired mercy, and not sacrifice, and the knowledge of AHYH more than burnt offerings. 7 but, like Adam, **they have broken the agreement**; they have acted like traitors against Me there.* 8 Gilead is a city of those who work iniquity, **slippery with bloodstains**. *9 and as troops of robbers wait for a man, the company of priests' murder in the way to Shechem; for they have done wickedness. 10 I have seen horrible things in the house of Jacob: the fornication of Ephraim is there; Jacob is defiled. 11 Also,* **Judah, a harvest is appointed to you, when I return the captivity of My people.** (Speaking of Shelanite-Judah).

Here is where I was shown what I think is the culmination of the message for now, and in direct connection with my two reoccurring dreams on this very subject: Beginning at verse 3 it became amazingly specific for me where my dreams are concerned. 16:3 & 4 in the dreams specific context were given as direct orders to me. *You will also notice a very positive trend occurring by the end of 16:14 which I believe harkens back to 16:2 - (Countries in league w/USA) will be crushed by their own doing. All those who ruled and destroyed WILL be removed!*

Isa 16:1 *"Send the fatted lamb you ruler of the land from the rock of the wilderness, to the mountain of the daughter of Zion. 2 Like a wandering bird chased from the nest, will the daughters of Moab* – [Countries in league w/USA] - *be at the cliffs of Arnon.* **[See note below]** - 3 <u>You</u>, render counsel, execute judgment; make your shadow as the night in the middle of the day; Hide the refugees; do not betray the wanderers. 4 <u>Let My refugees live with you; be a covert shelter</u> for them from the pillager: *for the oppressor is* gone, *the persecutor is finished, the oppressors are terminated out of the land!"*

16:13 ***"This is the prophecy that AHYH had spoken concerning Moab before.*** *14 **But now** AHYH has spoken, saying, **in three years**, like the term of the hired hand,* (See note below) *the glory of Moab (USA) will turn to disgrace, and in all that great multitude, there will be a very small remnant, very few.*

How will the oppressors and persecutors be terminated as expressed in 16:4? As I have always taught; by their own hand; they diligently created and marketed their own Revelatory playbook over 2000 years ago with the intent to fabricate said destruction upon us all. All the while unwittingly creating that program to fall upon them after they make their final, committed move towards implementation.

"And the kings of the earth, the princes, and chief captains, the rich, and the strong, and every bondman and freeman, hid themselves in the caves and in the rocks of the mountains – [Deep Underground Bunkers] *- And they said to the mountains and the rocks, 'Fall on us and hide us from the face of the One seated on the throne, and from the wrath of the Lamb."*

By their own hand!

Related details:

- *Like a wandering bird chased from the nest, will the daughters of Moab be at the cliffs of Arnon.* – This was telling me that although this "was" a prophecy for Moab "before", it is now shown to me as a warning for today - *13 This is the prophecy that AHYH had spoken concerning Moab before. 14 But now......*

- The "nest" for America will most likely be the coastlines and cities where most will run from. ***The "cliffs of Arnon"*** is important! Arnon was a river/cliffs that divided the Moabites from the Amalekites', a border. For America, this must be referring to the Mississippi and possibly also the Rockies.

- *make your shadow as the night in the middle of the day; hide the refuges; do not betray the wanderers, 4 Let My refugees live with you; be a covert shelter for them from the pillager:* – This is referring to making myself and the others with me unseen to anyone outside of our sphere at that time, to allow people in and to not betray them in any way, to be a shelter, etc. This is in direct accordance with two highly specific and reoccurring visions ongoing from 2010, but had little context for.

- 16:14 **But now** AHYH has spoken, saying, **in three years**, *like the term of the hired hand,* (See note below) *the glory of Moab (USA) will turn to disgrace, and all that great multitude, there will be a very small remnant, very few.*

Term of the hired man – This is a cultural reference meaning, that the hired man only works his very specific times, he starts and stops at exact times to which his pay is calculated. In verse 14 it is being used in the context <u>of this 3-year time frame as an absolute time frame</u> - not flexible. To me, at the time of these warnings, my inclination could only be at that time, that the start count for this 3-year period should be from the date the warnings were given, but now we finally know differently. *8/22/15.* The 22nd day here was not lost on me either, as 22 is the letter Tav, <u>the Last, the end - Finalization</u>!

However, now in 2019 when the warning of the 3-years came fully, which made the final timeframe for something catastrophic happening in the year 2022, now we see the greater probable meaning of that first date in 2015 and the number 22.

The closing section really hit me on that Sabbath, it tied all the others together for me. Until this part, I wasn't sure what I was being shown, but if you knew the details of my two reoccurring vivid dreams on this subject, everyone would see how this last part is so specific and important.

America is now both new Egypt and Moab! What most amazed me is how the texts give direct instructions on how I should act. Which means nothing to you unless you know the recurring dreams showing many people arriving here. In my awake times while thinking of such a possibility my initial reaction was more on the negative side prior to being shown these specific texts which came across a lot more like an admonishment. Giving me specific instruction on how to act at that time.

> "…. **You**, **render counsel**, **execute judgment**; *make your shadow as the night in the middle of the day;* **Hide the refugees**; **do not betray the wanderers**, 4 **Let My refugees live with you**; **be a covert shelter** *for them from the pillager:* **for the oppressor is gone, the persecutor is finished, the oppressors are terminated out of the land!**" [Obviously speaking of after]

Prior to this, albeit they were exceedingly vivid and specific dreams with great detail, having the two dreams recurring through the past 10-years wasn't exactly proof of a future event for me. I have never been wired in that overly, religiously dramatic way as to believe every dream or thought meant something important. This now makes them proof for me and gives me a specific time frame for those visions which I continually asked for, but didn't receive fully when this string of Sabbath's came. Now I must believe we have the data.

In summation: This information was only dispersed to very few individuals back when I received it. I knew it was for wider consumption and to be dispersed immediately to everyone within my sphere, but because I knew it would be taken as prophetic and also required me divulging the occurrence of my visions, which were obviously preparing me for things to come, I sat on it for over two years.

People should understand, I have been involved with deprogramming Christians and some Jews for a long time, and most of them have been so shell-shocked by the many false prophets and teachers that such an event or occurrence such as these visions literally must be ripped out of me before anyone will hear such a thing from my lips. I truly and quite literally become nauseous when I think of anyone considering me in the same light as any Christian prophecy teacher or Shelanite cartoon character, and this causes me to withhold.

If I had to read into all this a bit further, and again, based on two similar dream segments, my belief is many people will soon be forced to travel away from their homes. My location is about as far north as one can get in the US, so, many will be traveling north from all over, based on the dreams. I can also tell you from what I was told by one of the arriving travelers in the last, expanded dream segment, that those having to travel will be led concerning direction and who to look for. Led by whom? Use your imagination because I just cannot bring myself to spell it out here. I'm still two seconds away from hitting delete.

I would also remind everyone to process this and things which appear to be coming our way soon in the context of the Greater Exodus while the contents of Revelation are happening.

I will also remind everyone who has hopefully remained living inside the Eternal's Everlasting Agreement, to remain convinced and expecting the Fathers covering as needed. I know that part is the hardest, especially for the majority who have never been literally pulled out of an absolute death situation that left no marks and no way to explain it, but it does come.

"…. *then, my people, <u>upon whom my name is called</u>, <u>being converted</u>, will make supplication to me, and seek my face, and <u>return</u> from their transgression: then will I hear from heaven, and will forgive their sin and heal their land.*"

And if they do not KNOW His name and KNOW what to return to, then they better be covered by the Elect one.

The Second Warning
5/20/2017

The Nineveh Eclipse - 2017

So, someone sent the Revelation 9 text hereinafter seeing the information on the coming 2017 eclipse. I also saw an advertisement from some university, Tennessee I believe it was. Just could not believe it. It said –

It should have said...

Then I also found out that on April 8th, 2024 there is yet another *twin* eclipse over the USA that crosses in the opposite direction. I have to say that with the 2017 eclipse being so rare, that seeing another one just like it nearly 7-years later, made me think.

So will it be… — S. Asher

We don't have to go far to find people who believe that America is the mystery Babylon, although I believe that to be the Shelanite 'Judahites in Judea, and Jerusalem specifically. Personally, for me, prophecy is nothing more than the telling of what has already been and will be again – *A revolution of events!*

In the case of the USA, this makes us more like, first Egypt. It may be more accurate to see the USA as the *Greater Egypt*, and at the same time much like Nineveh. However, unlike Nineveh, the majority will not repent, but may even double down in their evil and try to fight back what they know is coming for them. And THAT will top off the cake by proving this place to be the Greater Egypt, when her second round of plagues, one thousand times worse than any Pharaoh has ever seen, come to her soon. With only those SEALED to survive and thrive through it and after.

Some yrs. ago I wrote a paper about Nineveh and sent it out. Unfortunately, today I cannot find it, so I will give my redacted thoughts out of my head herein.

If one goes through the history of Nineveh, they will find some major and direct correlations to the USA of today.

- Nineveh/Assyria was a military might and a serious bully.
- Nineveh maintained a well-known oppressive foreign policy.
- By their foreign policy and war machine, they extracted the wealth from the nations around them. (Sounding familiar yet?)
- On 6/15/763 BCE, Nineveh watched a total eclipse traverse the country. They, unlike Americans who are treating the event like a vacation destination, took it as a sign that "God", was mad.
- The Assyrian records that we have today say that their leaders and holy men said that their king would be removed from office. (Sound familiar?)
- Same records show that they also believed they were ABOUT to

- come under Gods judgment.
- Jonah's record says that all the "people" had already, by that time, began to break down emotionally fearing this. (The USA will not)
- Amazingly, about <u>3.5 yrs</u>. later in 760 BCE, Nineveh had a massive earthquake. (Much about a massive earthquake coming to the USA is being spread far and wide these days. Specific about the USA being split into 3 parts)
- After the quake, they had a famine and plagues.
- Also by that time they had experienced bad political turmoil and the larger northern countries were gearing up to invade them. (Again, same things we are hearing today)
- Then, when the people of Nineveh are sufficiently divided and fearful of all manner of geopolitical uncertainty, and just after their earthquake - In walks Jonah!
- Jonah tells them they have 40 days.
- Nineveh repents and is spared for a time.
- Then as I depicted in my Asher Codex, around 744 BCE they returned to their expansionist ways and by 721 BCE they killed and enslaved the entirety of the 12 northern Hebrew tribes.
- Then, by 612 BCE the Eternal One, through His mighty one Yehovah, allowed Babylon to take them out of play.

Exactly like America for some time now, the evil being pointed out against Nineveh was all about their nations violence against the weak.

They broke the Everlasting Agreement; they trampled the 1st law of free will on all fronts by their lifestyle, religious practices, and culture. And history records that by their military actions and foreign policies they were noted for great brutality, human slave trafficking - (Pedophilia rings), and general cruelty. All as it is recorded - done in the name of "raising revenues." ALL sounding very familiar indeed!

And if I left out the name Nineveh most anyone today would have thought I was writing about the USA.

Now, this is the warning:

Jer 6:1 *"O sons of Benjamin take refuge to flee out of the midst of Jerusalem. And blow the ram's horn in Tekoa; and set up a signal over Bet-ha'kerem. For* <u>evil appears out of the north, and great destruction comes</u>*."*

Jer 6:2 *"I will destroy* <u>the daughter of Zion</u>*,* <u>the beautiful and tender one</u>*."*

Jer 6:3 *"The shepherds with their flocks have come to her; they will pitch tents on all around her. They will, each one, feed in his hand."* [Meaning she is already surrounded]

Jer 6:4 *"Prepare* **war against her**. *Rise up and let us go up at noon! Oh! Alas! For the day wanes!* <u>**The shadows of the evening are stretched out**</u>.*"* [Meaning this happens AFTER summer]

> Jer 6:5 *"Rise <u>up and let us go up by night and destroy her cities."</u>*
> Jer 6:6 *"<u>The Elohim of legions has said,</u> '<u>**cut down her tall trees**</u> and pour out a mound against Jerusalem; <u>**She is the city to be visited**</u>"*

[The capital]. "In her midst is <u>oppression, throughout</u> her!"

[Tall trees=rulers) & Oppressive, free-will-killing laws, and Pedophilia]

Jer 6:7 *"As a cistern keeps fresh its waters, so she keeps fresh her evil.* **Violence and destruction are heard in her**. *Sickness and wounds are continually before My face.* **(DC)**

Jer 6:8 *"O Jer*USA*lem, take advice, that My soul not be alienated from you;* **that I not allow** *you to ruin, to be a land with not one alive in it."*

[Odd, first time, Jeremiah and others were left alive in it, as I am certain many others throughout Canaan were also left alive. So, this, in this future reference must be speaking in context directly to those tall trees and all who aid them]

Jer 6:9 *"So says the Eternal of Hosts; They will glean bare the remnant of Jacob like a vine. Send out your hand **again**, like a grape harvester over the shoots!"*

Again! As in THE second time! As in Jerusalem *then,* and somewhere else now; And SEE, it did NOT reference the capital of Jerusalem this time, it referenced the Hebrew lineages. As I have shown in my books, Ephraim, Josef and Judah have long been scattered into another place.

Jer 6:10 *"To **whom will I speak and give warning that they may hear? Behold, their ears are not open, and they cannot listen.** Behold, the Word of the Eternal is a joke to them. They have no delight in it."*
[Souls have been firewalled due to the blood on their lips and bodies]

Jer 6:11 *"I am filled with the prophecies of the anger of the Eternal. I weary holding them! Pour it out on the child in the street **and on the circle of the young men together**. For even the husband with the wife will be taken with the aged full of days."*

[I won't belabor this, but the Hebrew word used and horrifically mistranslated here as "circle." It is more specific to men being *secretively intimate* with each other.] [That understood, the entire verse states that no one is exempt anyway.]

Jer 6:12 *"And their houses will be turned to others, fields, and wives together. I will return My hand on those living in the land, declares the Eternal."* [As I depict in my books, Jeremiah goes into great detail on this point about how whole cities and towns will be empty, and how the Eternal One's people will be using the dwellings as they travel.]

Jer 6:13 *"For everyone from the least of them, even to the greatest of them **takes a profit; and from the prophet even to the priest, everyone deals falsely**."*

Jer 6:14 *"They have also healed the fracture of My people slightly, saying, Peace, peace, when there is no peace."*

Jer 6:15 *"Were they ashamed when they made an abomination? They were not at all ashamed, nor did they know to blush. Rightly, they will fall in great variety, as I oversee their stumbling!"*

Jer 6:16 *"So says the Eternal; **Stand on the road and seek, inquire of the Everlasting path, where this perfectly ordered road is, and attain a resting place for your souls**. But they said; We will not walk in it."*

Just like Jonah, what do you think Jonah's message was to Nineveh? Stop being mean? No! But, just like Jeremiah, the instruction, ultimatum, was to stop warring against His Everlasting Agreement from top to bottom. And when we do that, all the rest falls in line.

Jer 6:17 *"I **established watchmen over you**, saying; Listen to the sound of the ram's horn. But they said; We will not listen".*

Jer 6:18 *"So hear, you nations, and know, you assembly, that which is coming."*

Jer 6:19 *"Hear, O earth, Here I am! I draw evil towards these people, **rewarding their inventions! In as much, never attending on my words, My Instruction. They rejected it.**"*

Jer 6:20 *"What is this coming? Frankincense out of Sheba, and the good cane from a far land? **Your burnt offerings are not for acceptance, nor are your sacrifices sweet to Me.**"*

Jer 6:21 *"Behold! I am providing stumbling-blocks to this people, and the fathers and the sons together will stumble on them; a neighbor and his friends will perish."* - [By the Shayatim-Jinn!]

Jer 6:22 *"So says the Eternal; Behold!* **A people comes from the north country, and a great nation will be stirred from the sides of the earth.***"* [I am finding this last part – *Sides of the earth* – quite interesting. Think of how so much negative attention has been given to Antarctica of late, with Buzz Aldrin going there and saying that we are in unimaginable danger from something there. And think about how only on a flat earth can Antarctica be its "sides."]

Jer 6:23 *"They* **will lay hold on bow and javelin; they are cruel and have no mercy.** *Their voice roars like the sea; and they ride on horses, arrayed like a man for the battle against you, O daughter of Zion."*

Jer 6:24 *"We have heard the rumor of it. Our hands have dropped down; anguish has seized us, pain like one giving birth."* [Just Like Nineveh]

Jer 6:25 *"Do* **not go out into the field or walk by the way, because of the sword of the enemy and terror from every side.***"*

Harkening to the prophecies of the sealed ones remaining inside their dwellings for a time and being protected from the scourge without.

Jer 6:26 *"O daughter of My people, put on sackcloth and roll in ashes. Make mourning for yourself, as for an only son, most bitter mourning; for the ravager will come suddenly on us."*

Jer 6:27 *"*I **have made you a fortress among my people; you will observe and prove their path.** *"*

Jer 6:28 *"They are all rebellious revolters, walking in slander. All of them are like bronze and iron; they are corrupters."*

Jer 6:29 *"The bellows are charred; the lead is consumed from the fire; the foundries are fused and desolated; Their evil no longer lifted up."*

Jer 6:30 *"Men will call them silver slag, for the Eternal One has rejected them"*

There are many points in Jeremiah's texts that I feel are directly speaking to *this* country's imminent fall, and like the rest, as I have shown in this book to this point, they all tend to express the same thoughts and ideas, many even exactly the same.

As touched on earlier, it applies:

Rev 9:1 *"And the fifth angel trumpeted. And I saw a star out of the heaven falling onto the earth. And the key to the pit of the abyss was given to it. 2 And he opened the pit **of the abyss**. And smoke went up out of the pit, like the smoke of a great furnace, and the sun was darkened by the air, by the smoke of the pit. 3 And out of the smoke locusts came forth to the earth.* [So obviously this is NOT just smoke]
*"And ability was given to them, <u>as the scorpions</u> of the earth have the ability. 4 And **it was told to them that they should not harm the grass of the earth, nor every green thing, nor every tree,** except only the men who **do not have the seal** of God on their foreheads."*

There it is again! The seal of the Eternal One and those who have it.

Additionally, and as I expressed earlier, the ancients believed that it is a portion of the *Jinn* who was locked outside in the Abyss.

Considering the wording of that and other similar Revelation texts; Do the dark side love war and total destruction? YES! They have been pushing us towards WW3 for years now while doing their level best to destroy everything and everyone inside this snow globe right down to possibly the "matter" it is made from. My point is, they could care less about the grass and trees! So, as I stated before, these texts must be referring to something else. The answer - *The Yeshurim are the Earth, Grass, Trees and Green things!*

I realize that many people tend to become fearful when reading and considering the implications of such things, but I reiterate here again for the sake and wellbeing of those people: What were the three Messengers of the Eternal One told directly before entering the besieged city of Jerusalem where the majority of the people, under the permission of the king had been eating human flesh almost the entire time?

They were told to go in and SEAL all those who were actively against the king, *in their hearts and minds,* and against all that was going on in there. They chose not to pollute their bodies and souls with dead flesh & blood. And after the siege, after thousands and thousands died, with the rest hauled off to Babylon, Jeremiah and many others were allowed to go free, and even given local villages that, for some unknown reason, the Babylonian army decided not to raise, burn and salt along with the rest of Judea. And what agricultural features does it say they would find in those hamlets? Fruit and vegetable fields! If the Eternal One want's you saved, you will be saved. And if for some reason He does not, then what can we do about that, and who are we to question it?

At that time, in Judea and specifically behind the walls of Jerusalem, UNDER the worst conditions those people, knowing the original law, decided to die and allow their loved ones to die if need be before they would annihilate the Everlasting Agreement and corrupt their souls. Are you also ready for that? It should also be noted, that Jeremiah, like Daniel, was already living the Agreement for a very long time before that.

I have shown within my first two books that the 1st law is the seal upon your right hand and your forehead, and I explained what that means. So, if in our time it is truly to be that much-alleged *end-times,* then you should all expect a Greater Exodus into safe zones after being passed-over in your dwellings.

I truly wish that there was a way for me to get such a warning out much farther and wider than I am currently able to. But then again, the prophecy is already clear; *who can He send that they would hear, and what could he say that they would consider?*

    Not me. I was already told more than once to stop praying for these people. So, what good would a verbal warning be? My guess is, because of the times we have lived in for so long, and with mass media and technology, the ways that we have to gain information and or purchase any book on any subject in mere seconds only to have it dropped on our doorstep days later; the warnings have long been easily available to all, especially so inside the USA.

Their ears are shut because of their assimilation of false religious and other narratives, and their souls cannot prompt them loudly enough because of the blood that permeates their bodies and beliefs.

It is very difficult to know what may come, while also knowing that you have their way out, but relegated to watch it happen. But then again, that is what the prophets were for. All anyone has to do is hear.

The Third Warning

The Warning: To All American Rulers, Clergy and False Prophets!
5/27/2017

The word of the *Eternal One* came to the Prophet Micah the first time concerning the Sons of Jacob, specifically. Now it's relevance appears to have come again at a time when the context for it has been revealed after the first two previous warnings by Jeremiah and Jonah.

I will try to keep this as short as possible and leave the additional reading up to all of you individually. My advice would be to go read Micah, although most English translations are horrific, then return to the first prophetic warning herein, then again to the second.

The 3rd warning is also a blessing to all of those who live within the confines of His *Everlasting Agreement*, and I also believe it to be a "near" blessing to all the "elect" who are not in yet but will be.
Meaning, Christians and everyone else outside of it, BUT, who have not participated in the evil escapades of the fallen or their human sycophants by that time, in full knowledge.

The "warning" part of this, although unknown to most casual readers of Micah who were taught by the false teachers, priests, and prophets, is that this 3rd warning calls out and identifies all of the leaders within their disciplines as those who are marked for utter destruction. Again, the English versions don't make some of this easy for the casual reader.

The "Elect one" / Messiah:

This 3rd warning was also an answer to my personal question regarding the one I have known as the *Elect One,* and as Jews and Christians call the *Mashiach.* As well, it also came to me that these texts aid us in understanding more about how two Messiah's could exist in the end days; one evil, the other the Eternal Creator's man.

Of all my years of studying and crushing the Christian opposition concerning their incorrect interpretations within the Torah and prophets', specifically areas in which they believed to be speaking directly about Yehshua, this past Sabbath was the first time I saw something else.

- Mic 1:5 *"All this is because of the transgression of Jacob, against the sins of the house of Jacob. What is the transgression of Jacob? Is it not Samaria? And who caused the high places of Judah? Are they not Jerusalem?"*

This excerpt is out of an older, Stone Edition Tanak translation from the Hebrew which is very accurate, but most do not understand its greater meaning. *First,* only a very small part of this Prophets warning has anything to do with the Shelanite-Judahites; *i.e. the Babylonian-Judahites.* It is speaking to, and for ALL of the 12 tribe lineages of Jacob who resided in the north of Canaan. This warning, which had its place in his time, is also a far future warning as well, exactly as I have shown you to be the case with *Jeremiah, Jonah, Isaiah, Ezekiel, Abrahim,* etc.

To understand this, one must understand that the Eternal One, through His prophet, is calling out NOT the land masses themselves of *Samaria* or *Judea*, but specifically the ruling hierarchies – *Government, Corporate & Religious.* Meaning, yes! The people themselves have their own level of responsibility as you will see pointed out later, but, the real issue then, and NOW, is with the rulers in several fields of endeavor who control the people and the narratives. **THIS 3rd warning is to all of them!**

So, you should now understand that it will be their "capitals" and "citadels" where those rulers, priests, and captains of industry will be utterly destroyed, flat!

They will be wiped away by some catastrophic events. Flattened, tilled under like farmland, with all of their graven statues, obelisks, and monuments crushed completely. However, they already know this and have been preparing for it for many, many years in America and around the world.

Meneh-Meneh-Tekal-Upharsin!

They are known to have been building deep safe-zone bunkers to hide in. Mirroring every single major government office required for the continuity of government from DC, too deep underground installations in Denver and other areas from Colorado to New Zealand. Their work in Colorada was finalized in 2010.

The Eternal One via His mighty ones is telling all of those evil doers through His prophet, <u>assuring you all that your bunkers will not save you</u>! But will be the final resting place where your evil bodies are tormented to death and dissolved while your souls are caught and quarantined forever.

- Mic 1:13 *"Tie the chariot to the stallion all those living in Lachish; that was the origin of sin for the people of Jacob; it was in you that the sins of Jacob were uncovered!"*

This is important and another point most miss completely. *Lachish* was the first city that embraced all of the death cult practices of Ba'al. From *Lachish,* this destructive death cult spread out all the way to Washington DC, and from that harlot into all the capitals and corporations of the earth.

Speaking directly to all of the establishment who brought in the original sin narratives; from politicians to religious leaders, to the false money, banking establishment, etc. NONE will be left out, forgotten or missed. The sickle swings, and soon it comes!

- Mic 2:1 *"Woe to those plotting wickedness and preparing evil on their beds! In the light of the morning, they carry it out because it is in the power of their hand.*
- Mic 2:2 *"They covet land and take it! They covet homes and take them! They oppress a man, his household, even a man's inheritance!*
- Mic 2:3 *"So the Eternal One says this: 'Behold, I am plotting evil <u>against this family</u>, from which you will not remove your necks; nor will you remain exalted, for it is an evil time'.*

Plotting against this family? Interesting. Because of the Bilderbergers, and all of the other "few" families who believe themselves to be one family to rule all souls, must be who this speaks of.

- 2:7 *"My ways are benevolent <u>with the ones who walk in Uprightness</u>!*

The Hebrew here for the word "uprightness" is (Yasher). The root word (asher) having much the same meaning, which is *"upright or straight".* Meaning, **in character.** I show you this portion of the texts because this is the portion that was highlighted to me prior to reading the entire context.

- 2:12 *"I will surely gather all of you, Jacob! I will surely assemble the remnant of Jacob! I will place them together like a flock in a fold; Like a herd in its pen <u>they will teem with people</u>!"*
- 13: *"<u>The One</u> who breaks forth [birthed] will go before them; they will break out and pass through; they will go out through the gates; <u>their King</u> will pass in front of them, with the Eternal One leading!"*

These prophetic texts really show me something in light of the <u>Bethula</u> <u>astrological sign</u> coming up to birth the Mashiach star over a three-day period on Sept/23rd/24 & 25th 2017. Jews historically understand this as the *Jupiter planet being berthed as the Mashiach planet and sign – aka - "The suffering Mashiach"* But more was opened to me on this particular point on this day.

Jews continue to believe that their Mashiach (Elect one) to be a man that will arise from within their ranks to take care of and handle all of the many issues among men that no man has ever been able to do, and of course, to put them in the seat of authority above all nations, etc. *Their version says* this is NOT a man/messiah figure who has ever lived before or someone that they have known, or can know beforehand. But the prophets gave a different description.

Soon you will see that they have one major issue with their story. This is one of the many reasons why the false Judah has never listened to our "Hebrew" prophets, and why they have long deemed them to have no authority.

- The prophet says; *"Now listen you leaders of Jacob, you officers of the house of Jacob! Is it not up to you to know the [original] law? Rather you hate good and love evil! You remove peoples skin from them and the flesh from their bones! You have eaten the flesh of My people, you have stripped their skin from them and broken open their bones! You have sliced them up for the pot, like meat in the cauldron." Then, they will cry out to Yehovah, but he will not answer them; he will hide his face from them at that time, just as they had done their evil with their deeds!"* **(Mic 3:1)**

Do I have to spell that out? Just because our leaders have chosen evil does not mean that many of them are not originally part of the greater tribes and house of Jacob. As the prophet points out to them in this 3rd warning, THEY SHOULD HAVE KNOWN THE LAW!

However, so goes the way of free will! They CHOSE evil over good, and death over life. They chose to be led far away by the evil fallen ones who taught them as they taught myriads of others before them, to *"Spirit cook"* our children for their own empowerment. To torcher infants and adolescent children before sacrificing them to glean their *Adrenochrome* saturated blood. It has always been about the shedding of blood! It cries out from the drenched ground still! Nothing has or will change on that front.

Remember, when the second eclipse comes on April 8/2024 moving in the opposite direction to the previous Aug/21st/2017 eclipse, it appears to be making its epicenter crossing over a spot where human blood sacrifices were held for thousands of years! Yet another sign to the blind as to why this will all come to pass!

The (X) falls on Southern Ohio in an area called – Little Egypt!

The Eternal one through His prophets shows how the priests and prophets who have always misled His people, *Jacob,* have always asked to be paid for their services; He tells us through His prophets today when this all kicks of.

- 5: *"Therefore, it will be night for you because of your visions, and darkness will come on you because of such divination; the sun will set upon these prophets **and the suns light will be blackened**!"* – [Jonah!]

- 6: *The seers will be ashamed, and the prophets disgraced, and all of them will have gags on their lips because they had no word from The Eternal One!"*

- 8: *"But as for me, I was filled with strength by the spirit of Aheeyeh, and with justice and strength to inform Jacob of his transgressions and the house of Jacob of his sin!*

- 9: *LISTEN NOW! To this O' Leaders of the house of Jacob and the officers of the house of Jacob who detest justice and who twist all that is straight, who build Tzion with blood, and the Capital with iniquity!*

- 11: *"Her leaders judge for bribes, and her priests teach for money, and her prophets, prophecy for money! Yet they alleged to rely on the Eternal One, saying, 'Behold, the Eternal One is among us! No evil will come to us! Thus! Because of you, all the Capital* [Tzion] *will be plowed under like a field! Jerusalem* [Capitals] *will become heaps of rubble, and the temples like stone heaps in the forest!* [Old Stone Tanak Trans]

In Chapter 4 it begins with yet another depiction of "Greater Exodus Speak", for all of Jacob, both those previously *"Yeshurun" - "Yasher"*, and all of the Elect who were not, but now brought into camp and taught the path; those who finally decided to listen to what the two witnesses told the world. And, just as was provided to Abrahim in his time, we apply the law of the in-grafting of souls.

Also, I now tend to believe that it may just be Yehshua that is being spoken of in this prophesy as we also see in chapter 4. However, if one continues to see the greater view of this prophets' future, end-of-days, understanding, there will be many who must not have been "elect" or "Yehshurun" at all. They will be taken off to be slaves somewhere else, but as in the days of Assyria, they are somehow set free to return.

Is this a sign of the Beacon-Seed effecting the Drone population?

(See Beacon-Seed; Asher – 2018)

Chapter five brings us back to where I started this in regard to the "Elect one" or Mashiach.

- Mic 5:2 *"And you, <u>Bethlehem Ephrata</u>, being least among the thousands of Judea, but from you, <u>he will emerge</u> for Me to be ruler over Jacob; and <u>His origins will be from ancient times</u>, <u>from the days of eternity</u>". Therefore, he will deliver them* [Jacob] *from their enemies <u>until</u> the time **that the woman in childbirth, gives birth**; Then <u>the rest of his brothers will return</u> with the children of Jacob."*

- 3: *"He will stand up and lead with the power of Aheeyeh, and the majesty of the name of Aheeyeh, his mighty one!"*

- 4: *They* [Jacob & Elect] *will settle in peace because at that time he will be known as great to the ends of the earth. This will assure peace."*

So, I can understand how much of the Christian NT data may be given as literal astronomical signs, rather than the physical signs of a man, and in other cases vise-versa. However, knowing the Hebrew texts as I do and knowing the grammar, etc., I see no other way to understand this other than being a direct reference to a physical entity. The Jews also believe this to be that as well, however, these Micah texts completely eliminate their version of it being some yet *unknown* man to emerge as a great world leader of geopolitics and religions, etc.

No way!

"*Bethlehem Ephrata - <u>His origins will be from ancient times</u>, <u>from the days of eternity</u>". - He will deliver them* [Jacob] *from their enemies <u>until</u> the time **that the woman in childbirth, gives birth…**"*

[Until that time? That *sign* occurred on Aug/21/2017 -aka- *Asher-8* in conjunction with the American eclipse, sign of Jonah.]

Now, recall the Apocalypse of Abrahim's texts which clearly made this same point!

It would appear his origins are KNOWN! *To everyone!* And *from ancient days/times! And from the days of (Olam!)* = Eternity.

Come on! AND THEN it provides us the sign of Bethula? The birth of the Mashiach star? That said, we should also remember that this star/birth constellation occurs annually. *So, for sure we need more than just that to know when the actual event year is coming.*

Either way, if you do not have or know the corrected Creator's Calendar, you will never know where and when to look for any of this. **Be advised,** this will occur in the 1st month, the month of Neftali!

The orthodox Judahites could not have been more wrong on so many levels! This may be the first time in my life that I admit that the Christians got something correct. This must be referring to a human-Mashiach-soul entity that has already been here and been known widely. And also, an entity (Elect-one), that has been around and in this specific service to **Aheeyeh – the Father**, for a really long time, exactly as the book of Enoch clearly depicts him as being- (Olam!) Which if memory serves, the Christians believe all that about Yehshua.

Shocking news for the *Fallen-Followers* of Shelanite-Judah: In my mind now, this solidifies exactly *where* and from whom that so-called anti-Christ will arise. If he exists at all. *Meaning,* if this prophecy squarely pinpoints Yehshua as this Elect one who leads Jacob in the end-days and after that, then the alleged and much awaited Babylonian-Jewish Mashiach that comes has to be the imposter!

Proven by the fact that he never existed before, and that no one has ever known of him prior to then.

Look at this part again - *He will deliver them* [Jacob] *from their enemies <u>until</u> the time **that the woman in childbirth, gives birth**…..:*

UNTIL – Doesn't the Christian religion believe that in some way Yehshua is connected to, or have the ability to restrain a certain level of absolute evil from breaking forth upon the world? I am sure I have heard that taught before in some fashion. Well, this prophesy is clearly saying that this "man from ancient times", having the power of Aheeyeh, has been restraining certain evil enemies – delivering Jacob – from enemies – <u>UNTIL the sign of Bethula is fulfilled during the month of Neftali</u> – *The Lamb/Shepherd sign!* At which point my best guess, being based on all of the Noah event dates as previously depicted herein, is, that all hell quite literally broke loose before that day. And, from THAT time forward, being within the Sabbatical 7th-year, no further assistance will be required in that way by him or his legions.

And in what year will that most likely kick-off? **In 2022!**

As I mentioned already, the sign of Betulah is an annual event. So, the fact that the prophetic texts speak of this sign several times must also mean that this sign is being used "by the Eternal & Hosts" <u>as a countdown</u> to the final "Age."; *Meaning*, they know the day and hour because only they know how many annual rotations of that sign have been allotted to us. We should think of that sign as being a burning fuse!

The Damascus Connection:

Amazingly, today Assyria [Syria] remains an underlying issue for the USA and the world. Is it also just coincidental that the center of all adversity centers in the area of *Mosul?* **Which is also known as ancient Nineveh!** Yet another coincidence? Is not Damascus Syria yet another *lit* prophetic *fuse* that we are waiting to see blow?

THIS IS THE WARNING TO THE ELITE RULERS, JUDGES, PRIESTS AND ALL WHO FOLLOW YOU! CERTAIN AND FINAL DESTRUCTION HAS ARRIVED FOR YOU AND YOURS!

Meneh-Meneh-Tekal-Upharsin!

Yehshurim, find solace in the facts laid out prophetically as I have shown you in my Greater Exodus book and here with Micah that you will find safety and provision as in the days of Noah and Moshe!

- 6; *"The remnant of Jacob will be found in the middle of many peoples like dew from Aheeyeh; like raindrops on grass..."* etc.
- 7. *"And the remnant of Jacob will be among the nations, in the center of many peoples...."*

Micah tells us clearly and emphasizes specifically how all of the contributors of evil within the halls of government and else ware will be completely threshed out and ground to dust; that **all** of their cities, man-made idols, statues, obelisks, satanic Eshturah tree groves, etc., will be plowed under. Later shown in chapter 6 that no death cult rituals such as burnt offerings and such were ever asked for or expected; *meaning*, this restrains the overall context; *meaning,* that this is the reason for the warning then and today.

Moving on to explicitly state that He only asked us to love justice, act with love and kindness and to be humble. These once opulent rulers and religions charlatans will now scrounge for food and delicacies that were once at their fingertips, all stolen from the sons of Jacob and the elect, and they will find none!

My thinking is, these are the ones that the higher elite never invited into their deep bunkers. One set of people will die slower than their masters, but both will die out!

- 7:2 *"The devout people have disappeared from the land, and the upright* [Yasher] *among men is no longer here.'*
- 7:15 *"<u>As in the days when you left Egypt</u>, I will show you wonders."*

In the end, all the nation's leaders, sub-leaders, Kings, the mighty men, the priests and false prophets who petitioned for money, and every sycophant who followed them will be ground to dust. Then, the nations will hate themselves, be brought low, and most importantly, they will be afraid of all those who will then make up the renewed, house of Jacob!

Hos 10:6 *"It will also be carried to Assyria, a present to King Jareb. Ephraim will receive shame, and Jacob will be ashamed of his own counsel* – **[Rulers].**

Hos 10:7 *"Samaria is cut off; her king is as a bough on the face of the water. 8 Also, the high places of Bet-Aven, the sin of Jacob, will be destroyed. The thorn and the thistle will grow up on their altars. <u>And they will say to the mountains, Cover us! and to the rocks, Fall on us</u>!"*

Rev 6:16 *"And 'they said to the mountains' and to the rocks, "Fall on us," and hide us from the face of the One sitting on the throne, and from the wrath of the Lamb* – [Elect one] - *17 because the great day of His wrath has come; and who is able to stand?"*

As it is written, so shall it be; All of the top people who have followed their unanointed false god will find no refuge within the many, massive Deep Underground Bunkers they built for themselves with the sweat stolen from us. They will be overheated, burned and choked to death by the lava breaking in, and finally buried by the stones they paid for to save them. While their lower counterparts perish in various and sundry ways above ground. A fitting end.

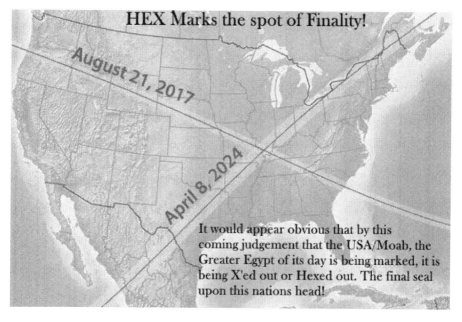

As I pointed out previously, the Hebrew letter (Tav) is the last 22nd and final letter in the Hebrew alphabet, and it also carries with it the numerical value of 400 and the deeper meaning of *Mark* or *Sign!*

I won't belabor this point too much, only to point out that in the more ancient Hebrew alphabet this letter (Tav - ת) was actually shaped in the form of an (X).

I firmly believe that these two celestial events wherein the land will have been *Crossed out* by darkness, to be a very deliberate *sign* **and** *mark* on this place, and not as a blessing. Prepare!

So will it be… S. Asher

The Fourth Warning
6/16/2018

The following is for clarification. Originally, I believed this was only meant for me, as a kind of a hand-off for a more direct aid package for some soon coming events. However, many have inquired of me on this exact topic and continue to appear to have been thrown off by what appears to be a change in my understanding on this matter, however, that is far from the case. I have added this warning as a deeper clarification on this topic.

First, understand, that when I have taught in the past through my books, and specifically, wherever I spoke on the subject of the NAME and entity of Yehovah, and how he has been presented in most texts, along with how the masses have been made to misunderstood his position, etc., in my own books and teachings, *which were meant for new people returning to the original 1st law path,* I have always been forced to edit my data as to not overwhelm and cause the reader to be side-tracked on to yet another religious bender, or shut-down.

Each book is specific to its overall revealing and understanding of the "PRIME" Eternal Creator, *His law, His name, your return path to Him and it,* and nothing more. Had I continued for the sake of my own ego and ability to overwhelm the reader with my detailed knowledge in these areas, those new returnees would not have remained on the most important road in their new walk at that time. Because of this misunderstanding with many readers new to this path, most everyone who learned from me does not always have clarity on this nuance concerning the entity known as, *Yehovah.*

My goal has always been to shift people over to the Prime Eternal Creator source, **Aheeyeh**, and His original 1st law of the Everlasting

Agreement so that their souls could finally be released from this captivity. This greater emphasis towards *Aheeyeh* and His law appears to have caused some people to shift certain other important relationship activity and their attention away from the more localized gatekeeper and arbitrator of the 2nd law - (Yehovah).

These previous points about how I teach must be understood in case you are now feeling a bit confused on this whole "seek Yehovah" thing while comparing this understanding with anything I have provided in the past. THIS is NOT a change, but an extension for those who are ready and may soon need it. The greater nuance of our renewed relationship with *Aheeyeh* at the SOUL, spiritual level now, and especially for when we separate from these bodies, compared to how the greater system works and **who** oversees the physical realm that we currently occupy, may have been lost on many. There was a time for that level of data, and now it appears this is the time for this connection. What for? We can only speculate given that it was provided to me couched in 6 very specific warnings so far.

Those who Return to *Aheeyeh* through the 1st law have their soul forever covered by Him. They have a renewed soul-tether connection back to Him to receive spiritual, enlightened updates, spiritual instruction, hearing His voice in us, and to be protected and transported directly back to Him when that time arrives in the physical.

In this physical reality which is generally governed by the 2nd law of destruction by the entity known as *Yehovah*, and among all those who consent to remain rebels to the 1st law, he has always been the warden, the judge of guilt, and the executioner for all who break the 2nd law.

This is how we all know he has been depicted throughout the bible texts, but most generally the writers of those texts tended to lay their poor choices and guilt at *Yehovah's* door. **Meaning** – The devil made us do it! *Or,* The LORD YHVH told us to kill this and sacrifice that, etc. Unfortunately, they, as well as everyone after them knew full well the 1st law and the 2nd law, and of their consequences. They made their own laws loosely based on the 2nd law, listened to only their own intellect and ego's, and falsified the voice of the only mighty one that they had any contact with. It was easy for the false one, the imposter Satan to guide them away from even that 2nd law.

We have ample proof of this through all the texts showing how they never truly received any of the major blessings as promised by the Malakim of *Aheeyeh* had they only consented to return to Him in that wilderness. But did receive fairly constant chastisement and destruction via *Yehovah* for breaking that 2nd law. This is what the record shows.

What is not so obvious to people who **find**, **return** to, and **live** the path of the 1st law is, that this *Yehovah* entity is also the overseer (in closer proximity) of all those righteous Yehshurim people (in this physical world) who are NOT rebels to either law. Since by returning to the 1st, we also fulfill all of the 2nd law by default, as well.

Remember – "I have not come to destroy the law, but to fulfill it…"

Well, now you understand what he was saying there.

Following are the texts used to depict this next warning:

Ruth 3:12-13 – "*now, while it is true that I* [Aheeyeh] *am a redeemer,* there is also another redeemer closer than I. ¹³ *Sleep the night, and in the morning,* if he [Yehovah] will redeem you, *fine! Let him redeem; But if he*

[Yehovah] *does not want to redeem you, then I will redeem you—as (he) Jehovah lives! Lie down until the morning.'* (Stone Edition Hebrew Tanak)

This is how these segments were shown to me, and NOT meant to be understood strictly within the normal context of the Ruth story. This was a message, and that means there will be a need for it sooner than later.

All who have learned from me should already know that there exist 3 voices throughout the Tanak. In the early Exodus, from Mt Horeb to just before Mt. Sinai we see the voice of the Malakim/angel of AHEEYEH attempting to get them all on track with His 1st law – *The Everlasting Agreement.*

You can now see below via the Ex-23 texts – AFTER they fully rebelled against the 1st law *and regardless of the mixed-up context order that I have long proven to exist after Exodus 19*, we clearly see it refers to a change in management, along with the new voice speaking - the 2nd Malakim that will be sent to them from the 1st voice which was the Messenger of the Eternal One. This second entity eventually gives them the 2nd law that they and every LIVING Physical bodied soul after them will be forced to comply with regardless of the later superstitions that the religious world cast upon your mind between then and now.

Exo 23:20 "*Behold, I am sending* an Angel before you, to guard you in the way, and to bring you to the place *which I have prepared*. ²¹*Be on guard before him and listen to his instruction. Do not be rebellious against him, for he will not forgive your transgressions; for My name is in him.* ²² For if you fully listen to *his instruction*, and do all *which I speak*, **I will** be an enemy to those distressing you, and will be an enemy to your enemies.

Ex-23 *is* when this event occurred! From that point on the ONLY physical human/souls who have NOT been UNDER or condemned by that 2nd law are those few in every generation who find their way back to the 1st law. *Plain and simple.* As I have always said, if there are 2 laws, then there have to be 2 peoples!

If you also recall, I used the words of Yehshua in my Land of Meat & Honey book, via the Essene texts, which clearly show Yehshua teaching them about the Pharaoh-sees SECOND law and how innumerable they are. Most importantly, Yehshua speaks of a long known ancient Hebrew proverb of sorts, which paraphrased here, is Yehshua telling them how, when MOST of the children of Jacob and their mixed multitude rebelled against the 1st law as Moshe provided at that time – [which were 7], that Moshe begged with the Malakim of AHEEYEH to not allow His people to be destroyed - *left unprotected and provisioned* - AND, that Moshe asked the Messenger if he could give the rebels ANOTHER law, one that they could more easily live with and comply with so that LATER, EVENTUALLY, they could RETURN to the 1st law and be saved, etc., etc.

Continuing – Yehshua told them that Moshe explained to the Malakim – *'Is it not better for a man with a broken leg to walk with a crutch until he is healed, rather than to just allow him to fall and die by the way...'* etc... To which, amazingly, the Malakim of AHEEYEH complied with his request for another, interim law. After that, they got the prison warden and purveyor of all pain and blessings, *Yehovah* to deal with. THAT is exactly what you are seeing coming into play here in Exodus 23. And exactly what you have seen within the confines and systems of this entire world ever since. Most of the world is still walking on crutches and just barely at that. THIS is why I have used Yehshua's great parables of the wheat and tares so many times in my books. Because as I have shown you correctly, how those parables are speaking specifically to all those wheat – Yehshurim – in each generation who get harvested, and get OUT of this system. While all the darnel/tares get *Reaped* and recycled back into this system for another try. THAT is mercy my friends, clear and simple. THE CRUTCH!

TWO voices – TWO mountains – TWO laws – TWO peoples eventually becoming ONE people again while walking on crutches!

Ruth 3:12-13 – *"now, while it is true that I* [Aheeyeh] *am a redeemer, there is also* **another redeemer** *closer than I.* ¹³ *Sleep the night, and in the morning,* **if he** [Yehovah] *will redeem you, fine! Let him redeem; But if he* [Yehovah] *does not want to redeem you, then I will redeem you—as* (he) *Jehovah lives! lie down until the morning."* (Stone Edition Hebrew Tabak)

NOW, the big question seems to be HOW do we separate the two in prayer or otherwise. This, of course, will have to be an individual thing, and surely you should go to the Father – AHEEYEH – and ask, but as I have understood this and how I believe I explained in that 5th warning article, we should look at it like they are in two columns. We go directly to the Eternal Father in prayer for all things and especially for knowledge, wisdom, discernment, and everything to do with our immortal soul, as He is the keeper of all souls and the keeper of all things eternal and within those eternal realms. And then, move those prayer requests, needs, thanks for aid, etc., **in the physical world** to Yehovah since he is the localized keeper/redeemer of the realm for this time. – *"there is also* **another redeemer** *closer than I."*

Recall what the Malakim Gabri'el said to the prophet Dani'el concerning the time differential between the Eternal One hearing his requests and them actually arriving on the scene to aid the prophet?

Since I mentioned that third voice again, maybe some added explanation on that 3rd voice is due.

Basically, you can apply most of what you have learned in Christianity here about the Satan entity being an *imposter type*. And, as I recently re-explained in my *Beacon-Seed* book, that entity has on many occasions, and as seen throughout many Bible stories, pretended to be the voice of the Yehovah entity or his angel entity to many people. His aim as always was to sway people through suggestion or direct order away from the known laws, either the 1st or 2nd law or both, to hurt those people.

Although most people do not correctly understand the exact relationship they see occurring in the opening of Job, that is another place that we can identify this Yehovah entity or the angel of Yehovah, but also the Satan entity AND the other "sons of God" in one place while we also see them referring to THE Eternal Creator in their conversation. I believe I lined all this out using the actual texts in my Soul Revolution book to make the point there as well. Another major point that most are not even aware of pertaining to the opening pages of Job is, that the scene being witnessed there is not actually happening on earth, but somewhere else. The older narrative is that the "sons of God," as depicted there in Job, are actually the 24 Elders in heaven, with Yehovah, and that they are entertaining the Satan entity on some points of interest. This may be true, but it does not change the greater meaning as I have taught it many times now in my other books. But, something else to consider.

That said, this is an important question that I haven't paid much attention to through the years. And proving Yehovah as being that literal *angelic entity* which has long been reconfigured in the minds of men as being GOD himself, would again, change many of the books storylines and the meanings of many details as you may have seen me go through, added clarity. However, whether he *is* a Malakim of AHEEYEH or he is the local mighty one who controls other Malakim locally, neither configuration in my mind would change the way we present ourselves to the Father in prayer and thanksgiving, *vs* how we correspond with the *Yehovah* entity for our needs in the physical realm. All homage goes directly to the Father and ends with the Father, and NOT to any other entity. Presenting yourself with reverence to a local and powerful entity for aid or blessing *i.e. Yehovah* is NOT the same as worshipping the ONE Eternal Creator. It may seem like a fine distinction at first, but I think with practice and by thinking it over some, the distinction is achieved.

The moral of this story is, even though you know and have a relationship with the President of the company, while his VP has been put in charge of all internal issues, don't end-run the VP taking all your hopes, dreams and issues to the Pres. Or risk being ignored by the VP while attempting to navigate a lifetime of evil people/souls, demons and destruction to come in this physical place for now. *'there is one that is closer...'*

The rest of these warnings consists of reading:

- RUTH-3 *and*
- JOEL-3

The 5th Warning
11/17/2018

This is regarding and in sequence with those 4 warnings from 2015 which appear to be just over the horizon now in 2019. These Isaiah texts are also in sequence after showing people the 4th warning comprised of Ruth 3 and Joel 3, along with other texts which built off the initial 4 warnings. All of them, from the first four warnings to this one appears to have a quickening pace and escalation of events about them, not the opposite. These later warnings appear to be a further escalation and even appear to be providing an actual time frame and three locations worldwide. But, the key to knowing the true times from any point for any of these prophetic warnings, will be to know when to start the countdown. At the time of receiving the first six, I did not yet have that start date.

READ Isaiah 21 below: I do not believe any versions you may have will read the same.

Also understand that Isaiah, like Yonah, did not like the message he received and didn't want to deal with it. What he was not considering or allowing to be part of his process was that Free will is the other half of the equation. Yonah only saw that he had to go in and tell the leaders and all the people that they were about to die, with a lot less emphasis on the (if you change) part of it all.

Also understand, that although we read our prophets and believe them to have been real and true connections with the Eternal One, that does NOT mean that the WAY these prophecies come to pass will be in the ways we have been taught or imagined by those who know far less than us, *or,* that the prophecies won't be orchestrated to occur by the evil ones themselves using technology, and not the Creator or His gatekeeper Yehovah at all. As I have posited in the past many times if it was the United Nations that signed the paper for the STATE of Israel to be born in ONE DAY, does that mean it's NOT the fulfillment of that prophecy? **Being the Last or Terminal Generation!**

At no time has it been shown HOW a certain prophecy would be fulfilled in such detail (outside of the GE prophecy that is), nor have the other prophecies made it clear WHO would make it happen. In the end, it is the Eternal One who allows all these things to happen through the free will of all those involved and all those not directly involved by their tacit consent.

Additionally, it is his Warden, Yehovah, who allows these free will choices to play out in this physical creation for now. So then yes, it is in fact prophecy fulfilled, at least in part because where the ancient State of Canaan is concerned, it is the 2nd and much Greater Exodus that will finally be the completed fulfillment of all that. But for now, it has been fulfilled as required for all the steps to the end to be fulfilled. Of course, there are many other prophecies as well, all converging to one pinpoint end, although I do not believe that most understand any of them correctly. Just as many of you may still say that the current State of Israel is in no way relevant prophetically and totally man-made, etc. Flat out, you are 100% wrong and not understanding the big picture. No, it is not the final and complete fulfillment, but it is the portion required to start the end-time clock running.

The following English is taken from my older Stone Edition Tanak and has a far better translation than any other English I can find.

Isa 21:1 *"A prophecy concerning the wilderness <u>of the West</u>! 'Like windstorms sweeping through the desert, it will come from the wilderness, from a fearful land."* **[Antarctica?]**

Isa 21:2 *"A hard vision was spoken to me; The treacherous one will act treacherously, and the destroyer will destroy. Go up, O Elam! Besiege O' Media! I have brought an end to every sigh."* [Meaning, the nation who overstepped on all nations causing them harm and anxiety has been brought low – America]

Isa 21:3 *"Therefore, my loins are full of anxiety, Pains have seized me as pains of a woman in childbirth. I am bent down from hearing it, and terrified by seeing it."*

Isa 21:4 *"My heart has become disoriented; panic has terrorized me. He (Yehovah) <u>has turned my festival evening into a horror!</u>"* [Timing clue – Which Jewish feast is this?]

Isa 21:5 *"<u>Setting the table, lighting the candelabra, eating, drinking,</u> 'Arise you officers and spread oil on your shields.'"*

[Interesting, the Hebrew uses a very obscure word here for multi-candle holder – *candelabra*. BUT, in all the English version except for the Stone Tanak, they totally left this sentence out! I tend to believe this depicts Chanukah. December!]

Isa 21:6 *"For thus said my Adonai to me: 'Go, station the watchman, and let him tell what he sees.'"*

Isa 21:7 *"He will see a chariot, a pair of horsemen, a donkey chariot and a camel chariot; and he will listen intently with much to hear! And he will call out like a lion!"*

Isa 21:8 *"My lord, I stand on the watch-tower constantly during the day, as well I am stationed all the nights';*

Isa 21:9 *"Behold! It is coming! A chariot with a man, a pair of horsemen.' Each says loudly – It has fallen! Babylon has fallen! And all the statues of its gods have been shattered on the ground!"*

Isa 21:10 *"It* [Babylon] *is grain on the threshing floor, for Me to thresh! That which I have heard from Yehovah of legions, mighty one of Jacob, I have declared to you!'*

The next phase and location to be affected:

A prophecy concerning Dumah: = *The land of Edom, whose homeland was called Seir. It is also understood that the "watchman" they call out to is Yehovah the gatekeeper.*

Isa 21:11 *"He calls out to me because of Seir: 'Watchman, what of the night? Watchman, what of the night?'*

Isa 21:12 *"The watchman said, 'Morning is coming, but also adversity! If you truly desire it,* [the light], *repent and RETURN!'*
[Ahhh…and there you have it! The Watchman of all LAW, the 1st law, and his 2nd law for those who continue to rebel against the 1st; clearly telling them to RETURN to the law of they truly desire to be saved.]

The 3rd phase and location to be affected:

A prophecy concerning Arabia:

From early on in this book I eluded to the prophecy that states how the worst time of troubles will last <u>*only about one year*</u>, this is it. I tend to believe as I stated earlier, this must be the time that was shortened for the sake of the Righteous and Elect.

Isa 21:13 *"In a forest in Arabia will you lodge, you caravans of Dedanites.* [This is important because it is depicting that all the people in Arabia today will be forced to move out]

Isa 21:14 *"Bring out water for the thirsty! Those who live in the land of Tema greet the wanderers with food.*

Isa 21:15 *"For they will wander because of the sword, because of the drawn bow, and because of the severity of war.*

Isa 21:16 *"For thus said the lord to me: 'Within a year, as with the year of a hired man, all the glory of Kedar will be ended.*

Within a year? As with the hired man? I have explained this ancient understanding before. The "hired-man" time frame is absolute. Am I to understand all this to mean "within the year" for us in these three localities?

Again, if we are looking at it kicking off heavily in 2022, then this one years' time frame continues to fit within the entirety of the Noah prophecy time frame of events based on our calendar.

Isa 21:17 *"And the remainder of their army, the mighty heroes of the sons of Kedar will be diminished, For Yehovah, the mighty one of Jacob, has spoken!'*

All's well that ends well, I guess.

For someone that is. Someone who has been SEALED!

The Sixth Warning
12/22/2018

Joel

Read the following verses in order as if they were written that way.

FYI: Joel is very important, which is most likely why most translations are horrible. The chapter & verse segments are completely wrong, with most versions only having 3 chapters. For instance, the correct Hebrew or English should have 4 chapters laid out like this:

Chap-1:1 to 20 – Chap-2:1 to 27 – Chap-3:1 to 5 and Chap 4:1 to 21:

If yours does not have it this way, burn it, because that means a large chunk of Joel is missing entirely, and one can only imagine how flawed the rest of that translation version is.

When reading these verses and others, understand that the prophet knew who he was referring to as he spoke the prophecy. We know that the texts were manipulated because one entity, *like Yehovah*, should not be found referring to himself in many cases like he's another entity entirely, much less in the same paragraph.

Joel 1:13 *"Gird yourselves, you Priests, and wail you ministers of the altar; come spend the night in sackcloth you ministers of **my** Eternal One, for meal-offering and libation have been withheld from the temple of your god!"*

Joel 2:13 *"Rend your hearts and not your garments, <u>and **return** to Aheeyeh your Eternal One</u>, for He is gracious and merciful, slow to anger and of great kindness, and He relents of evil."*

As with most of the prophets, and as I have shown to be the case in my *Land of Meat & Honey* and *Greater Exodus* books, this call from the Eternal One through His many prophets for all to make "Teshuvah – Return" to their first estate, remains consistent. As does the punishment for those who ignore that call, and far worse for the teachers of falsehoods who steered most generations away from the truth.

Joel 4:13 *"Extend the sickle, the harvest has ripened! Come and trample [the grapes], the winepress is full, and the vats are overflowed – their evil is great!* **End of message:**

Again, we also identify the difference in character between the entities. No doubt that Yehovah can also be gracious, merciful, kind, etc., just not how we see it usually working out with him. *Aheeyeh*, on the other hand, has no choice but to remain that way forever, NOT changing. That is why the "closer" redeemer is needed so that the Eternal One can remain detached from the broad spectrum of evil that remains here until it is finally swept away by Yehovah.

Now read from Joel 4:14 to the end for context and make the entity distinction starting in verses 14 to the end.

- 14 – *"for the day of <u>Yehovah is near</u> in the valley of final decision…'*
- 15 – *"And <u>Yehovah will roar</u> from Tzion and emit <u>his</u> voice from Jerusalem."*

- 16 – *"But Yehovah will be a shelter for his people and a stronghold for the children of Jacob".* [The Yehshurim]
- 17 – *"Thus, you will know that I am Yehovah, your mighty one who dwells in the holy mountain, Tzion…."*
  [Tzion, from the ancient Hebrew "Siyyon", meaning Fortress/Citadel or Castle]
- 18 – *"And it will be on that day that the mountains will drip with wine, the hills will flow with milk and all the streams of Judea will flow with water, and a fountain will go out from the* house
  [People] *of Aheeyeh, and water the valley of Shittim.*

Older Stone Edition Tanak translation.

I have found and added a copy of chapter 4 on the following pages. This translation version is not great, but they at least got the chapter and verse division correct. I only made two minor corrections.

Joel Chapter 4 יוֹאֵל

א כִּי, הִנֵּה בַּיָּמִים הָהֵמָּה--וּבָעֵת הַהִיא: אֲשֶׁר אשוב (אָשִׁיב) אֶת-שְׁבוּת יְהוּדָה, וִירוּשָׁלִָם.

1 For, behold, in those days, and in that time, when I will return the captivity of Judah and Jerusalem,

ב וְקִבַּצְתִּי, אֶת-כָּל-הַגּוֹיִם, וְהוֹרַדְתִּים, אֶל-עֵמֶק יְהוֹשָׁפָט; וְנִשְׁפַּטְתִּי עִמָּם שָׁם, עַל-עַמִּי וְנַחֲלָתִי יִשְׂרָאֵל אֲשֶׁר פִּזְּרוּ בַגּוֹיִם, וְאֶת-אַרְצִי, חִלֵּקוּ.

2 I will gather all nations, and will bring them down into the valley of Jehoshaphat; and I will contend with them there for my people and for my heritage, <u>Jacob, whom they have scattered among the nations</u>, and divided my land.

ג וְאֶל-עַמִּי, יַדּוּ גוֹרָל; וַיִּתְּנוּ הַיֶּלֶד בַּזּוֹנָה, וְהַיַּלְדָּה מָכְרוּ בַיַּיִן וַיִּשְׁתּוּ.

3 And they have cast lots for my people; and have given a boy for a harlot, and sold a girl for wine, and have drunk.

ד וְגַם מָה-אַתֶּם לִי, צֹר וְצִידוֹן, וְכֹל, גְּלִילוֹת פְּלָשֶׁת; הַגְּמוּל, אַתֶּם מְשַׁלְּמִים עָלָי, וְאִם-גֹּמְלִים אַתֶּם עָלַי, קַל מְהֵרָה אָשִׁיב גְּמֻלְכֶם בְּרֹאשְׁכֶם.

4 And also what are you to me, O Tyre, and Zidon, and all the regions of Philistia? will you render retribution on my behalf? and if you render retribution on my behalf, swiftly, <u>speedily will I return your</u>

retribution upon your own head.

ה אֲשֶׁר-כַּסְפִּי וּזְהָבִי, לְקַחְתֶּם; וּמַחֲמַדַּי הַטֹּבִים, הֲבֵאתֶם, לְהֵיכְלֵיכֶם.

5 Forasmuch as you have taken my silver and my gold, and have carried into your temples my good treasures;

ו וּבְנֵי יְהוּדָה וּבְנֵי יְרוּשָׁלִַם, מְכַרְתֶּם לִבְנֵי הַיְּוָנִים, לְמַעַן הַרְחִיקָם, מֵעַל גְּבוּלָם.

6 <u>the children also of Jacob and the children of Judah</u> have you sold unto the sons of Jevanim, that you might remove them far from their border;

ז הִנְנִי מְעִירָם--מִן-הַמָּקוֹם, אֲשֶׁר-מְכַרְתֶּם אֹתָם שָׁמָּה; וַהֲשִׁבֹתִי גְמֻלְכֶם, בְּרֹאשְׁכֶם.

7 behold, I will stir them up out of the place where you have sold them, and will return your retribution upon your own head;

ח וּמָכַרְתִּי אֶת-בְּנֵיכֶם וְאֶת-בְּנוֹתֵיכֶם, בְּיַד בְּנֵי יְהוּדָה, וּמְכָרוּם לִשְׁבָאיִם, אֶל-גּוֹי רָחוֹק: כִּי יְהוָה, דִּבֵּר. {פ}

8 and I will sell your sons and your daughters into the hand of the children of Judah, and they will sell them to the men of Sheba, to a nation far off; for Yehovah has spoken.

ט קִרְאוּ-זֹאת, בַּגּוֹיִם, קַדְּשׁוּ מִלְחָמָה; הָעִירוּ, הַגִּבּוֹרִים--יִגְּשׁוּ יַעֲלוּ,

9 Proclaim you this among the nations, prepare war; stir up the mighty men; let all the men of war draw

So will it be... S. Asher

near, let them come up. כֹּל אַנְשֵׁי הַמִּלְחָמָה.

10 Beat your plowshares into swords, and your pruning-hooks into spears; let the weak say: 'I am strong.' י כֹּתּוּ אִתֵּיכֶם לַחֲרָבוֹת, וּמַזְמְרֹתֵיכֶם לִרְמָחִים; הַחַלָּשׁ, יֹאמַר גִּבּוֹר אָנִי.

11 Come quickly, and come, all you nations round about, and gather yourselves together; cause your mighty ones to come down! יא עוּשׁוּ וָבֹאוּ כָל-הַגּוֹיִם מִסָּבִיב, וְנִקְבָּצוּ; שָׁמָּה, הַנְחַת יְהוָה גִּבּוֹרֶיךָ.

12 Let the nations be stirred up, and come up to the valley of Jehoshaphat; for there will I sit to judge all the nations round about. יב יֵעוֹרוּ וְיַעֲלוּ הַגּוֹיִם, אֶל-עֵמֶק יְהוֹשָׁפָט: כִּי שָׁם, אֵשֵׁב לִשְׁפֹּט אֶת-כָּל-הַגּוֹיִם-- מִסָּבִיב.

13 Extend the sickle, for the harvest, is ripe; come, tread you, for the winepress is full, the vats overflow; for their wickedness is great. יג שִׁלְחוּ מַגָּל, כִּי בָשַׁל קָצִיר; בֹּאוּ רְדוּ, כִּי-מָלְאָה גַּת--הֵשִׁיקוּ הַיְקָבִים, כִּי רַבָּה רָעָתָם.

14 Multitudes! Multitudes! In the valley of final decision! <u>For the day of Yehovah is near</u> in the valley of final decision. יד הֲמוֹנִים הֲמוֹנִים, בְּעֵמֶק הֶחָרוּץ: כִּי קָרוֹב יוֹם יְהוָה, בְּעֵמֶק הֶחָרוּץ.

15 The sun and the moon are become black, and the stars withdraw their shining.

טו שֶׁמֶשׁ וְיָרֵחַ, קָדָרוּ; וְכוֹכָבִים, אָסְפוּ נָגְהָם.

16 And Yehovah will roar from Zion, and emit his voice from Jerusalem, and the heavens and the earth will shake; <u>but the Yehovah will be a refuge unto his people, and a stronghold to the children of Jacob</u>.

טז וַיהוָה מִצִּיּוֹן יִשְׁאָג, וּמִירוּשָׁלִַם יִתֵּן קוֹלוֹ, וְרָעֲשׁוּ, שָׁמַיִם וָאָרֶץ; וַיהוָה מַחֲסֶה לְעַמּוֹ, וּמָעוֹז לִבְנֵי יִשְׂרָאֵל.

17 So will you know that I am Yehovah, your mighty one who dwells in the holy mountain Zion; then will Jerusalem be holy, and there will no strangers pass through her any more.

יז וִידַעְתֶּם, כִּי אֲנִי יְהוָה אֱלֹהֵיכֶם, שֹׁכֵן, בְּצִיּוֹן הַר-קָדְשִׁי; וְהָיְתָה יְרוּשָׁלִַם קֹדֶשׁ, וְזָרִים לֹא-יַעַבְרוּ-בָהּ עוֹד. {ס}

18 And it will come to pass in that day, that the mountains will drop down sweet wine, and the hills will flow with milk, and all the brooks of Judea will flow with waters; <u>and a fountain will come out of the house of **Aheeyeh**</u>, and will water the valley of Shittim.

יח וְהָיָה בַיּוֹם הַהוּא יִטְּפוּ הֶהָרִים עָסִיס, וְהַגְּבָעוֹת תֵּלַכְנָה חָלָב, וְכָל-אֲפִיקֵי יְהוּדָה, יֵלְכוּ מָיִם; וּמַעְיָן, מִבֵּית יְהוָה יֵצֵא, וְהִשְׁקָה, אֶת-נַחַל הַשִּׁטִּים.

יט מִצְרַיִם, לִשְׁמָמָה תִהְיֶה, וֶאֱדוֹם, לְמִדְבַּר שְׁמָמָה תִּהְיֶה; מֵחֲמַס בְּנֵי יְהוּדָה, אֲשֶׁר-שָׁפְכוּ דָם-נָקִיא בְּאַרְצָם.

19 <u>Egypt will be a desolation, and Edom will be a desolate wilderness, for the violence against the children of Jacob</u>, because they have shed innocent blood in their land.

כ וִיהוּדָה, לְעוֹלָם תֵּשֵׁב; וִירוּשָׁלִַם, לְדוֹר וָדוֹר.

20 But Judea will be inhabited forever, and Jerusalem from generation to generation.

כא וְנִקֵּיתִי, דָּמָם לֹא-נִקֵּיתִי; וַיהוָה, שֹׁכֵן בְּצִיּוֹן. {ש}

21 And I will hold as innocent their blood that I have not held as innocent, when the [lord] – **Messiah,** lives in Zion.

Joel – Sixth Warning
Part Two
12/29/2019

THE WALL Event:

I originally sent this out early to a few people thinking the issue was a ways off, and for their aid in monitoring this issue since I don't have time to watch everything. I HAD NO IDEA that this issue was even a real issue yet, much less so imminent. I received the news links *below* only to find out that this is truly an actual, geopolitical issue rising quickly.

Pertaining to the horrific events to come and in regards to the 7 previous warnings; I finally asked for the **HOW** and **WHEN**, and He gave it to me. And if I am understanding this correctly, then we are seriously close to it all.

NOTE: Also keep in mind that this may coincide with the dollar reset and at a time when anything can happen to weaken the USA making invasion easier. Communication and Power outages; banks closed; food stoppages; fuel stoppages; coordinated mil strikes; etc.

APPLY THE PREVIOUS NOTE AS YOU READ THE FOLLOWING:

Joel 2:1 *"Blow a ram's horn in Zion, and shout an alarm in my holy mountain. Let all those living in the land tremble. For the day of Jehovah approaches; it is near, 2 a day of darkness and gloominess, a day of clouds and thick darkness, as the dawn spread out on the mountains,* <u>*a great and a strong people, such as there has never been the like, nor will there ever be again to the years of many generations;* 3 *a fire devours before it, and a*</u>

flame burns behind it. The land is as the garden of Eden before them, and behind them is a desolate wilderness; yea, <u>also there is no escape to them</u>."

2:4 *"Their appearance is like horses; and as horsemen, so they run. 5 They will leap like the noise of chariots on the tops of the mountains, like the noise of flames of fire that devour the chaff, as a strong people set in order for battle. 6 Before their face, the people will be pained; <u>all faces become red</u>. 7 They will run as mighty ones; they will go up the wall like men of war.*

They each go on his way, and they do not change their path, 8 And each does not press his brother; they each go in his path. And if they fall behind, their weapon they will not be stopped.

2:9 *"They will rush on the city; they will run on the wall; they will climb up on the houses; they will enter in by the windows, like a thief."*

2:10 *"The earth will quake before them, the heavens will shake. The sun and moon will grow dark, and the stars will gather-in their light."*

2:11 *"And Jehovah will give his voice before his army, for his camp is very great. For he who does Aheeyeh's Torah is strong. And the day of Jehovah is very great and terrifying, who can endure it?"*

A Point to consider when reading Nehemiah 3 – Nehemiah is nothing but the journal of temple **WALL building** progress. However, the Eternal knows me and what I know, and He used this text for one specific reason because He knew I would understand one *word/name* that would stand out right off to me in the Nehemiah text. Problem is, that name means nothing to anyone else in the context in which I tend to use it, so I must explain.

As trivial as it may seem, I have frequently used this name – JERICHO – while speaking to people about potential coming events, *i.e. (Operation Jericho – The Jericho Protocol – A Jericho Event, etc.)*, Kind of like a code to friends when speaking on the phone about certain potential eventualities, etc. *I have used this term in this capacity since around 2007 to be understood as "strikes" on major cities.*

Thus, the Eternal One brought me to this totally unrelated book of *Nehemiah,* to show me two totally unrelated things - (Unrelated in biblical times). And He did so only because of how <u>I personally understand and have used that name in relation to</u> **the EVENT** that this "Jericho" name was connected to, in a TV series by that name.

Did you ever see the TV series, Jericho? If not, go watch it on Netflix and pay seriously close attention to all the background in the scenes, and especially to the maps shown that depict which cities got destroyed, and how they got destroyed. THAT is what that name has signified to me since I first watched that series when it was new. **Destruction by fire is what it means. And from enemies from the South & North. As prophesied.**

The first part of Nehemiah provides the answer to how the prophetic Joel 2 events occur, and why.

Neh 3:2 *"And next to him worked the men of <u>Jericho</u>...."*

Neh 4:1 *"But it came to pass, that when Sanballat heard <u>that we were building the wall</u>, he was enraged, and took great indignation, and mocked the Jews. 2 And he said before his people and the army of Samaria; 'What do these feeble Jews? Will they fortify themselves? Will they sacrifice? Will they finish in a day? Will they revive the stones out of the heaps of the rubbish which are burned?'*

The timing of being shown these individual and unrelated texts in such a series, at the time in US history when the Trump wall project has literally inflamed our people and entire countries against it, makes me believe that Trump's wall is the impetus for the coming [Sennah'Charibe] attack. *Meaning, that the full-on commencement of that wall will be the sign of the "Jericho" event to come soon after, which is Joel-2.* [Note: As of 4/4/19 we are hearing that Russian military is moving into Mexico and down through to Venezuela, along with Chinese military.]

At first, I believed that the WALL **commencement** event [as lamented vigorously by Sennah'Charibe] would be my que to warn everyone, of not only the Jericho event about to take place but also that the Greater Exodus might be right on its heels. But it appears by the news I am seeing today, 4/5/19, that it may be sooner, then later.

It should be further understood that there really isn't any other way to have told me so specifically HOW this would happen <u>using biblical texts</u>. Had I not previously formulated my own personal connection between this *Jericho* name and in connection with such a specific and modern technical event, I do not see how He could have directed my attention to such a specific thing while also having me consider what I was seeing as being authoritatively from Him.

Connecting me and my modern day "Jericho event" understanding to one single and totally unrelatable spot in Nehemiah is seriously random.

I know how all this sounds, as well as what the previously given warnings make me sound like, but anyone who knows me personally knows 100% that I am NOT that guy. Like I said in the first warnings; *I didn't even want to send them out because I cannot bear to appear like the rest of the prophecy "experts" out there.*

As I have always said regarding anything I or anyone else teaches; Look hard and long at it all. Take your time reading between all the lines and always remembering to KEEP IT SIMPLE!

I have always been fully convinced of how I receive the info I get. And, that HOW I get it proves, *to me anyway,* to be originating from a source other than *me, myself* and *I*. But, I am NOT pushing anyone else to believe the info or that I am in any way more special than anyone else in all this. Just like the specific data in my books, I am compelled to tell certain things and that's all. I am NOT compelled to convince anyone of anything. Certainly, if any or all of this data comes true at any future time, then I do hope you all took it seriously, remembered it and moved accordingly. But I am not invested in your belief of anything. None of this has been fun for me. But I DID ask to KNOW it ALL many years ago. And without knowing at that young age, that, in knowing it, also came a responsibility that could not be put down. Ahhh, youth! Will we ever learn to just keep our thoughts to ourselves and our mouths shut?

Everyone better covet the Sabbath's and days we have left in peace. That may end for a while, soon.

SEE INFO AND THE JERICHO TV SERIES MAP BELOW which were sent to me from MICHELE A. You will also notice that on most, if not all US. Gov't disaster planning maps by govt agencies, that they tend to depict Montana as always outside of the affected zones. Even in the fictional TV series.

US Southern Border To Become New "Hot Zone"

Trump Issues "Declaration Of War" Warning After US-Mexico ... Conflict Death Toll Soars Over 280,000

http://www.whatdoesitmean.com/index2633.htm

So will it be…

The Seventh Warning
אזהרה אל שלוש שנים!
Zahar al Shelosh Shaneem!
Warning of three years!

"Upon o the high mountain, hoist a flag, raise a voice to them; wave a hand, and let them come to the doors of the nobles..."

READ Isiah 13 – 14 -15 & 16: Because it may soon be upon us all!

Isa 16:14 – *"In three years, like the term of a hired man. The honor of Moab (USA) will turn to disgrace, and then there will remain a VERY small remnant,* **not many!***"*

Isa 13:4 – *"The sound of commotion is inside the mountains like the sound of an enormous people, like the crescendo of the kingdoms of gathering nations; Yehovah, master of legions, is assigning officers for the legions of war. 5 They come from a faraway land, FROM THE END OF THE HEAVENS, brought by Yehovah as his weapon of anger to devastate the entire land!"*

This 13:4 text does not at all appear to me to be speaking of a standard military force as we know them to be. It is also evident that they are NOT coming from INSIDE of our Antarctic-ice-containment-ring. This force is something coming from outside of our protected area. The commotion from inside the mountains at first might appear to be speaking about earthquakes, and it may be. But, if the latter verses are not referring to human armies from this place, then that commotion, if we keep it all in context with itself, could be where these forces from the END OF THE HEAVENS are coming from and through. **i.e.** Through the mountains; as in, portals.

13:6: *"Wail!! For the day of Yehovah is near; It will come as a sudden attack from the Almighty One! 7 All hands will become weak and every person's heart will fail. 8 They will be terrorized; aches and pains will seize them, they will be in travail as a woman with child. Each man will be shocked seeing his friend; their faces become inflamed – (red-highly agitated). 9 Behold, the day of Yehovah is coming; a day of cruelty, rage and burning anger to make the land desolate; He will annihilate the sinners from it!"*

First off, we once again need to identify that the mighty one doing all the "Destructing" is Yehovah and NOT Aheeyeh. With that, we clearly see that this attack comes so suddenly and 100% by surprise to all, and the attackers so shockingly aggressive and destructive that all hands and hearts will give up hope. We can also see the description of a terror weapon that obviously DOES NOT KILL them immediately, but causes great pain, intense agitation and eventually killing those who it affects. **REMEMBER, those who are sealed by AHEEYEH will NOT be affected by anything to come.** And lastly, that ultimately, all "sinners" will be annihilated. Which does sound like a final, physical death.

NOTE: I do NOT believe any of this as described here and by other prophets, *one example would be in Revelation*, in which I believe the scorpions that sting and cause these same effects for 5 months is speaking about this same event; that none of what this enemy will do will be physical at all. I believe they will attack the brains/minds of most people which will, in effect, cause all of the above like a zombie apocalypse.

Isa 13:10, *"The stars of heaven, their constellations will not radiate their light; the sun will be dark at the time of rising, and the moon will not reflect its light. 11 I will visit evil on the land, and on the twisted ones their own lawlessness, and I will end the pride of the wanton, and bring low the ego of the strong. 12 I will make a man more valuable than rare gold, and people (in general) more precious than the gold of Ophir..."*

I do NOT believe (13:10-12) to be saying that the sun, moon, and stars should be taken as <u>literally darkened</u> as most will teach this to mean. I believe, given the fact that AHEEYEH will never remove these items from <u>our view</u> because we absolutely require them daily, that these kinds of texts are speaking more to the general feeling surrounding the stated events. **Meaning**, everything will be so utterly and unbelievably bad, in ways unimaginable to even conjure right now with our best Sci-fi imaginations, that everything inside or out will be dark in the deepest sense of that word to all those affected by this. ALL who DO NOT KNOW the NAME of the Eternal One, His law and have His SEAL upon them – **The 1ˢᵗ Law!** Which then brings us to – *"I will visit evil on the land, and on the twisted ones their own lawlessness..."* This word, *Lawlessness*, which is generally translated as "iniquity", is best translated as exactly that – LAW-LESS, "without the law." Which law? There can be only ONE! Now, all recovering Christians should harken their memories back to that horrific prophetic statement by Yehshua which he stated and obviously directed to ALL those who "thought" they believed and or understood anything he taught and or said, correctly; ***"Depart from me you who are LAWLESS, I never knew you..."*** OUCH! (Lawless = Without the 1ˢᵗ law of the Everlasting Agreement!)

13:15: *"Anyone found will be pierced, and anyone who is gathered up will fall by the sword. Their children will be cut down before their eyes; their homes will be pillaged, and their woman ravaged."*

13:20: *"It will not be inhabited FOREVER, it will not be settled from generation to generation; nomads will not pitch a tent there; nor will shepherds make flocks there. 21 Martens will lie there, and their homes will be inhabited by ferrets;* <u>Owls</u> *will live there, and* <u>demons</u> *will dance in it; 22 cats will howl in their mansions and jackals in their places of recreation. Her time* [Moab-USA] *is soon to come* [in 3 years], *her days will not long endure!"*

Anyone found will be pierced, and those rounded up will be killed off. Children included. Utter destruction that literally makes the entire landscape uninhabitable, forever! THINK **Reason** for Greater Exodus! ALSO: Who is doing this "finding, piercing and rounding up, etc.?" For me it is doubtful that these actions are being carried out by the forces who come from, THE END OF THE HEAVENS; Keeping it all in context with itself forces me to understand that all this is being done by those, "affected people."

14:1: *"For Yehovah will show mercy* <u>to Jacob</u>. *He will choose the sons of Jacob* **<u>again</u>** *and give them rest upon* **<u>their</u>** *land. And the* **<u>proselyte</u>** *will join them* <u>and be grafted into</u> *the house of Jacob...."*

Again, there is a myriad of prophetic texts which I have shown in my **Land of Meat & Honey** book and in other works which show us this same picture. Jeremiah killed it on this topic! And pointing out the "Proselyte" as being those who will be ingrafted to the tribes? – RETURNED to make TESHUVAH! I say that's kind of in your face. Who are the proselytes in our world? *Christians, Muslims, Buddhist to name the obvious ones will be the lion's share of ingrafted mixed multitudes who will be saved somehow, and long enough to be* *presented with the Everlasting Agreement to be CONSENTED to at that time.*

If you have not yet read the Land of Meat & Honey and the Greater Exodus books, in that order, now's the time.

Take care to read Isa 15 & 16 intently and understand it for our modern times:

16:13: *"This is the prophecy that Yehovah has spoken for Moab* **BEFORE**.... *BUT NOW, Yehovah speaks saying – 'IN THREE YEARS, like the term of a hired hand, the honor of Moab* [USA] will turn to disgrace, and there will be a VERY small remainder, **NOT many!***"*

THE 2019 1ST MEMORIAL DAY (March 13th) BEGAN THE THREE-YEAR COUNTDOWN

This warning of 3 years came to me about two months ago, and truthfully, at that time, I just ignored it because I thought that the previous 7 warnings in this same vein which began for me in 2015 to be enough warning to everyone. I really did not think anyone wanted to hear yet another thoroughly negative warning from me. Additionally, at that time and until this recent – PASSING-OVER event day, along with the High-Renewal-Memorial Day came where the legitimacy of the system was finally, fully confirmed to us, I did not see or understand fully yet the expanded meaning of this particular warning, and thus, thought it to be somewhat redundant to the other seven. Aheeyeh brought me back to this warning several times in those months because I was ignoring it. However, not yet being fully convinced of the calendars validity, I never even considered the two to be connected before this past Memorial. It took the passing and final vetting of the calendar system on this past memorial, with its checks & balances to snap this warning back into my mind, connecting the two. So, it all worked out, even with my procrastination.

The Sabbath day directly after the 1st Memorial of 2019, I was brought back to this Isaiah prophecy yet again, but this time it finally clicked – 3-YEARS! As previously stated, prior to fully vetting our calendar revisions and watching them work through the final two memorials of 2018, and passing those tests, and then through this year's first memorial which fell on the pagan Roman calendar date of March 13th, and also passing that test, was I finally fully able to embrace the calendar and be confident in its meaning, and most importantly, be confident about where and when this year's <u>FIRST day was</u>. Because, if you are following anything that I have been doing on this calendar issue for over ten years now, you should know that without the correct FIRST day of the new year, you are fully sunk for anything and everything after that. Aheeyeh clearly stated through His many prophets that He has HIS memorial days and everyone else has theirs, and He HATES all of theirs! So, if you are not finding and coming before Him on His days, you are and will remain thoroughly screwed; <u>especially where the coming prophetic events are concerned</u>! Nothing could be more tragic than screwing this up now via laziness or disbelief. I know His people, **the Yeshurim,** were always meant to know and have the original Creator timing system, and I also knew that He would have to show it to us <u>before the times prophesied in it</u>. *AS IT WAS IN THE DAYS OF NOACH, AND IN THE DAYS OF MOSHE, AND IN DANIEL, AND IN THE DAYS OF YOHANNAN.*

We count to 7-days and we count to 7-years! – [*See: The Creator's Calendar book 2019*]

As I show in the new Creator's Calendar book, we count the dark side of the moon phases for 7 years and then on the way back we count the lighted phases for another 7 years and vise-versa. <u>At this</u>

present time, we are counting the DARK side phases. Also, I believe the mechanics of the moon proved that we are in the 2nd year of the seven-year SHMITAH count as sighted on this past – Passing Over – event day/night.

There is some question that this latest Passing-Over event showed us a ¾ dark side moon phase and NOT the ½ phase as pretty much everyone else predicted it would be after last year's obvious ¼ Lighted side phase moon. Which, at that time last year, if it was clearly showing us a ¼ lighted side, then obviously the darkened side on that night last year had to have been a ¾ dark, which is exactly what everyone saw last year. But for now, let's put that aside. Because if all of us were wrong THIS year, believing we saw a perfect dark & light 50/50 moon phase, and it was ACTUALLY a ¾ dark side moon phase that we sighted, then we will know for certain by next year this time because if it was a ¾ dark side moon event this year, then next year it will HAVE to show us a FULL dark moon on that night, and no one can possibly mistake that.

ALL COUNTS BEGIN AND END, AND BEGIN AGAIN ON THE 1ST MEMORIAL

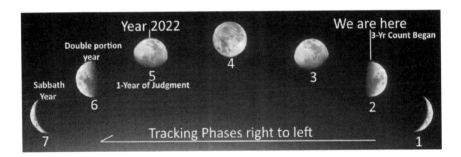

"Like the term of a hired hand..." In ancient understanding, this phrase has a concrete meaning to it. The "term" or "work time" of the hired man was exact. His start and stop times were exact! His

pay was based on this exact timing. As this term is used in the scriptures several times, it is always there to tell the reader that there is ZERO room for interpretation. THIS WILL be in 3-years' time (if) the start date is correctly known.

As I stated, this now became a significant warning to me because now I was finally provided a clarified and confirmed START date. Before having this start-date which renews itself on that exact same day each year without fail, I had no way of knowing or even believing that the Isaiah prophecy or the specific timing of 3-years as depicted in it, had any concrete meaning in our time. Now I believe I do. And after leaving me alone about this warning for months after bringing it to my attention over several Sabbaths, I continued to ignore the order to express it openly. Even on this past Sabbath day [after the 1st memorial], I was slightly surprised that I was brought back to it again, but this time with more urgency. And although I have these texts nearly committed to memory by now, I went ahead and reread them again anyway, but this time it all popped, the cogs meshed, and I finally saw the calendar connection. NOW I had the start date!

An End to hostilities:

In my original 7 warnings which began in 2015, but which I held back for two years until the context of those prophetic warnings became apparent to me in mid-2017, it is made clear that when the insane attacks and catastrophes come, that it will all **come and end in ONE years' time**! *(And if those days were not shortened, etc.)* THIS DOES NOT mean that other, lesser but also bad events will not precede this final year of utter destruction. Prophetic warnings of birth pains come to mind.

Will this 1-year period begin in 2022?

Will it begin at the mid-point of a new presidency? It could begin at that time and lead through the time of the 2023 Renewal Memorial rolls around. For me, it does appear that it will begin in earnest in 2022 for a one-year period, but I will have to watch closely and give this more thought, as should you.

Another point, and as I tried to express on the moon phase picture above, is that in the 6th year of this Shmitah counting will come the blessing year or ***Agricultural double portion*** year before the Sabbatical year where no crops/food can be grown. *Meaning*, His people (The Yeshurim) and all those who have become attached to His people, the mixed multitudes – (Elect) - will be provided double of everything they will need to survive in that 7th year. And, as per the Isaiah 13-14-15 & 16-chapter prophecies, along with several other prophets who present identical events, there will be no other people around anymore.

Additionally, within all of this, there will also be the Greater Exodus event leading everyone to some other unspoiled area of the earth which we will inhabit and prosper.

The year and number 2022 is also not lost on me. 22 being the final letter (Tav) in the Hebrew Alef-Bet. Having the meaning of - The END.

Another interesting and odd point that Nathan brought to my attention this week was that certain, and possibly all online calendar programs that allow you to skip ahead to see moon phases and to see how calendar dates line up in various years ahead, etc., seem to end, or not work past the year 2022. If anyone has the time to do more checking on that point, do let me know what you came up with.

The Beacon Seed are the "Upright Ones" Those hidden, protected, provided for and saved during indignations.

Gen 4:26 "Seth, he also bore a son, publishing his name, Enosh. At that time profanity was published upon the name of AHEEYEH."

After those days, and in the final days of Nimrod lived a man named Eber. Eber was the great-grandson of Shem who is known to have been a most righteous man. *Gen 10:21*

At that time, the original language being spoken was ancient Heber – *Hebrew*. Of course, this was the language brought down by Adam to Seth to Shem to Eber and beyond. The Hebrew language should be understood as synonymous with the lineage of Eber.

Eber and all his extended family members, in those days, are the only ones to <u>*not consent or comply*</u> with *Nimrod* where it concerned the building of his Tower-weapon. Today we call this weapon CERN. The following is a Genesis 11 excerpt from my yet unpublished - Asher Torah:

- 1 The whole earth was of one language and common purpose. 2 It was, as they migrated from the *front part, they found a valley in the land of Shinar; and settled there. 3 {They said}; Appoint each man among his neighbor, to put white clay in fire, to burn thoroughly, to be bricks of white clay; to build with asphalt which exists bubbling up. 4 They said: 'let us build us <u>a citadel, and a Pyramid to *shake the head of heaven</u>, <u>to advance our progeny; lest we remain dispersed upon the face of all the earth.</u>' 5 And AHYH descended to see the place <u>and the Pyramid</u>, which the children of men built. 6 And AHYH declared; if the people are united, altogether united, <u>and this</u>

piercing committed at this time; not everything will be inaccessible with that plan fulfilled. ₇ Come, let us descend there and mix their language that no intelligent hearing of a man to a companion remains. ₈ So, the Malakim of AHYH dispersed them from there upon the face of all the earth; and they failed to build the Pyramid. ₉ On there, the memorial is called out, *Confusion; because AHYH there mixed the languages of the earth; and from that time did they disperse them around the face of all the land.

* To SHAKE the HEAD of heaven? This corrected literal translation affords a very different picture of what was actually happening there. I submit that for one to (Shake) the HEAD of heaven = (GOD-AHYH or that which holds us inside this created place - the DOME); one would need a serious device or weapon-(CERN). I believe by the literal Hebrew context that this is exactly what they were building; a weapon to deploy against the "god" entity; but more likely a weapon to break through something to get out OR to let something back in and expand their progeny further as the context also implies in vs.4 We have to ask; where did they receive such knowledge to build anything that could have been such an obvious threat as depicted in the context, to the GOD-entity and us, as we derive from verse-6. *(Front Part) is generally translated as (The East), however, there is no evidence in the text for cardinal direction as we know to be East or Eastward. At this still early time in man's history on the land; the land mass was still one single mass, NOT separate Continents as we have today. Just prior to this time of Babel, the single land mass had already begun to split apart; {see Gen 10:25}, but still not yet completed enough to inhibit travel from (The Front Part), to the center, or the rear part as it were. * (Confusion) is the ancient literal translation of the word/name Babel.

Abrahim, formerly known as Abram, was also in the lineage of Seth, Shem, and Eber. As I have shown in my previous works, Abrahim was related to Noach and taught the understanding of the Everlasting Agreement by Noach. We also have this Torah reference to show he was known to be of the lineage of Eber.

- Gen 14:13 *"And one who had escaped came and told <u>Abram the Hebrew</u>; for he was living among the oaks of Mamre the Amorite, the brother of Eshcol and Aner. And these were possessors of an agreement with Abram."*

Abrahim was later visited by a messenger of AHEEYEH and told to walk "upright" – Yasher, seen from the texts use of the Hebrew word "Tameem".

- Gen 17:1 *"And when Abram was ninety-nine years old, Aheeyeh's messenger appeared to Abram and said to him; 'Aheeyeh is the Almighty God!' Walk before me and be **upright**;"*

Most western texts tend to translate that word as "perfect", however, remaining within the context of the whole story from Adam to Moshe and beyond, the far more correct translation, in this case, is "upright". Today we might translate it using the word Pious.

Walking, living upright is a direct reference to living within the confines of The Eternal One's Everlasting Agreement.

Two places that we can see both "Tam – Upright/Pious" and "Yasher – Upright/Straight" being used together, and in our oldest text is in Job 1:1 & 1:8.

אִישׁ הָיָה בְאֶרֶץ־עוּץ אִיּוֹב שְׁמוֹ וְהָיָה הָאִישׁ הַהוּא תָּם וְיָשָׁר וִירֵא אֱלֹהִים וְסָר מֵרָע

- Job 1:1. *"There was a man in the land of Uz, whose name was Job; and that man was **Pious** and **upright**, and one who feared God, and turned away from evil."*

וַיֹּאמֶר יְהוָה אֶל־הַשָּׂטָן הֲשַׂמְתָּ לִבְּךָ עַל־עַבְדִּי אִיּוֹב כִּי אֵין כָּמֹהוּ בָּאָרֶץ אִישׁ תָּם וְיָשָׁר יְרֵא אֱלֹהִים וְסָר מֵרָע:

- Job 1:8. *"And the messenger of AHYH said to Satan; 'Have you considered my servant Job, that there is none like him in the earth, a **pious** and **upright** man, reverent of power, shunning evil?"*

Job also provides additional verification for who is *not* Yasher. Giving a lengthy list of anti-social and destructive traits ending with their rebellion against His Everlasting Agreement.

- Job 24:13 *"They are among rebellers against light; they do not recognize His ways, nor do they stay in His paths."*
- Job 24:18 *"He is swift on the face of the waters; their part is cursed in the earth, regarding not way of the garden."* (Garden=food & reference to Edenic living)

Remember, we are connecting the dots from Adam through to the ongoing and mostly lost identity of those who I call "The Beacon Seed."

Unifying light

A most crucial point to remember concerning Abrahim and what the true Eternal One told him, vs. the many texts that contradict, is that anyone and everyone were to be welcome as home born when they came in and joined the compact of the Everlasting Agreement. As I have proven in other works, this had nothing to do with being circumcised, which was clearly an ancient sexual ritual brought forward by the Egyptians. There's more to it than that; an evil iteration laid into humanity needed to be dissolved from within. "Becoming" Hebrew was and remains more extensive than refraining from the murder and consumption of animals, or male circumcision.

With Abrahim and many of his lineage who lived previously, I believe there exists a hidden component that overcomes any lesser iterations that were added or manipulated by the fallen ones, and that works to infiltrate, overcome and protect our living souls, *and even those with no souls* [Drones] from something far more insidious. I also believe it is totally invisible to their evil prying eyes and, irreversible.

A highly spiritual seed lineage with some kind of physical DNA component to it. At least the false Shelanite cult and their scientists believe it does. They have been searching for all those infected by it for thousands of years and by any means. And history proves if one knows where and who to look at, that their main method to date, although varied, has been attempts at extermination.

The father of reassignment

Abrams name was changed to Abrahim - (Abraheem). To most, the plain reading of the texts tells them that his name was meant to depict his going forward as the *father of nations*. Abram having in it the ancient Hebrew word root for father; *Aba.*

However, as many have already learned through my other work, the (im) suffix added to Abrahm's name also has another, deeper meaning that was culturally relevant back then but lost on most today.

Correctly pronounced (eem), this suffix is most generally used in the Hebrew language to depict something plural. And really, in this case, it's addition does do that as well in a subtler way. The short version is, in our ancient Hebrew culture, the addition of the (im) - (eem) sound on the end of names or titles in ancient times was to turn that name into an obvious title of nobility.

The (eem) added to Abrahm was the outward marker provided to ensure that everyone from that day forward identified Abrahim to have the status of a king. So, having both the knowledge of the ancient culture, language and the texts as you previously believed you knew it, depicts all of these parameters to be working in concert all this time.

Meaning, the addition of the (im) to the root of the "father" portion provided us with the deeper understanding of great plurality – *Many!* Not many fathers, but as he should be more accurately known, the father of many "rejuvenated souls/people." While it's addition also proved useful as a nobility marker.

From that point forward his name was changed to Abrahim and never once after that in any text, by any later patriarch or prophet was his name seen pronounced in any other way. Unlike Jacob's alleged name change!

Here is only one proof of many that I used in my books:

Exo 3:6 *"And He said; 'AHEEYEH, the Mighty one of your fathers, the Mighty one of <u>Abraham</u>, the Mighty one of <u>Isaac</u>, and the Mighty One of <u>Jacob</u>. And Moses hid his face, for he feared to look upon the Eternal."*.

As you will see, and as I have expressed in other books, as you go you will need to replace the false term "Israel" when you see it in the Tanak for the name Jacob or the word *Yasher;* depending on the context.

And doing so will be in perfect order, because Yasher – *root word* "*Asher*", is known to be the singular form of "Yehshurun."

Yehshurun being a direct reference from AHEEYEH and His Messengers for all His Upright Ones!

- Isa 44:2 *"So says Aheeyeh, who made you and formed you from the womb. He helps you. Do not fear, My servant Jacob; and you, Yeshurun whom I have elected"*. (LITV Bible version)

Whom I have "elected?"

- 2Ch 7:14 *"and My people, <u>on whom My name is published</u>, will be humble, and pray, and seek My face, and turn out of their evil paths, I will hear from Heaven, and will forgive their offenses, and heal their land."* (MARKED as you will see)

That previous, single text alone is the beginning and the end of all arguments pertaining to WHO the Upright people of The Eternal One truly are. They are those who have His NAME published, attached, obviously connected to their lives! I can assure you, it is no other people alleged to be "special-chosen or saved."

On its face, 2nd Chronicles is speaking directly to and about a single, growing lineage of people that follow His original 1st law of free will exactly as foretold in the book of Enoch. (Greater Exodus – Asher 2012)

However, as we have already established by the original instructions provided to Abrahim, the idea was to enlist all comers to the path, and more importantly, mingling them to ensure the expansion of the Beacon Seed.

For there is no other logical or mathematical expression that could ever come close to accounting for *filling the earth* with so numerous grains of *sand* and *stars*.

To believe or even consider the idea that the Eternal Creator of all things seen and unseen would give Abrahim or any man such an extensive promise and compact having no intention of it being understood as literal or having a plan to carry it out in the natural and spiritual realms, leaves us with only two possibilities:

1. Epic short-sightedness brought on by manipulated Hebrew texts and falsification of cultural understanding. *or*
2. The entire story and idea are fake.

There are many historical and prophetic texts that depict a direct identification of those *Asher-Straight,* and *Yasher-Upright.* Although the readers of these texts always attach their meaning to be about them personally even while living their lives light years away from any correct understanding or implementation of them. Which is, that these are collectively the children of *Yehshurun –* The Water-Bearers!

Those who have been marked with His oil on their foreheads! Known and identified by their character which mimics His character via His original 1st law of free will. Walked out daily in the embrace and keeping of His Everlasting Agreement. Just ask Noach & Isaiah! Better yet, consult Yehshua! Didn't he tell you all about some special "oil" that some had, and some did not? The "oil" of some "light", some "spark" in connection with your soul?

While most of the peoples throughout the world today must by now carry the hidden, Beacon-Seed, few carry both the inward and outward markers.

Mark of the Beacon Seed

What is this Mark? We are creeping up on that. And later you will see just how the Babylonian Shelanite enemy cult has been hunting those who have it, and in our modern times have turned to science to find the Gene marker for it.

Eze 39:7 *"My name is holy, marking my people Yasher. Not allowing profanity on My holy name repeatedly! The heathen will know that I am Aheeyeh, the Holy One of Yasher."*

As we have learned through the years, The Eternal One is a bit particular about His name, that it is spoken on the blood-filled lips of anyone outside of His Marked people. The above verse has been corrected literally

An excerpt from the book – The Beacon-Seed - S. Asher ©2017

About the Author

Dr. Asher is a Hebrew Scholar who emphasizes the absolute, unapologetic distillation of all ancient data regardless of where it leads, or how much it hurts. His most recent work; *"Soul Revolution"* is a magnum opus queued up to eviscerate a plethora of ancient to modern superstitions and religious beliefs via in-depth correlations with ancient texts, prophecies, philosophy, and modern sciences. His latest book – *The Beacon Seed,* is meant to close the circle on the previous hidden original Torah precepts that he has re-unfolded to a quickly expanding population of seekers.

Although surpassing his original Karaite roots, Dr. Asher hails from an uninterrupted family lineage of Torah scholars originating in the Galilee area of Northern Canaan. Dr. Asher's teachings advance the original ancient Karaite philosophy of uncompromising Torah truth based on original Hebrew culture, traditions, and language while disregarding dogmatic religion and superstitions.

Dr. Asher spent most of his childhood in NY & NJ, continuing his learning in his early twenties in Israel where he became a citizen. During his formative years, Dr. Asher was exposed to the Christian religion extensively by those around him. Learning the Torah from the age of seven, he later quickly identified that most *Judeo-Christians* are deeply misinformed on all levels of Hebrew history, culture, ritual, and experience, and thus needed help. Understanding this from a youth, and knowing that it was the duty of all Hebrews - as mandated by the Eternal Creator - to become learned in His *'original Torah'*, apply it to their lives as a light to those around them, and then teach it to all who came in; he left no chance or circumstance to teach anyone who would listen.

In doing so Dr. Asher has dedicated himself to the teaching of the Eternal One's original law to all who wish to leave the worlds false religions and RETURN to the Creator's original path and truth which all souls originally left.

To that end, Dr. Asher formed the Ancient Hebrew Learning Center which has been the focal point for his online instruction. Those who glean insight from Dr. Asher include people from all religious faiths and social status. All of whom are people searching beyond fundamental religions for the more original truth which eludes them. His factual and hard-hitting teachings have been at times controversial because they have been lost for so long, yet enlightening and freeing to all who have embraced them.

Bibliography

Charles, R.H. *Book of Jubilees*. Trans. R.H Charles. Vol. 1. N/A, 1902.

Green, Jay P. *LITV Bible*. Vol. 1. Sovereign Grace Pub, 1985.

James, Montague Rhodes. *ABRAHAM, APOCALYPSE OF:* Trans. W. A. Craigie. Robinson's "Texts and Studies & Cambridge, 1892, 1892. <http://www.jewishencyclopedia.com/articles/364-abraham-testament-of>.

Stone, Irving. *Translator*. Ed. Rabbi Nosson Scherman. Trans. Irving Stone. 1 vols. Mesorah Publications, 1996.

Young, Robert. *Youngs Literal Translation*. Trans. Robert Young. 3rd. 1898.

Coming Works by Dr. Asher

The ben'Asher Torah
A literal and highly corrected translation of the Torah books known to be attributed directly to Moshe.

Midian to New Egypt
A fact-based fictional story depicting how the Hebrews and mixed multitudes of people leaving Egypt truly lived, rebelled and were split between Mt. Horeb and Mt. Sinai; their religious and cultural separation into two peoples, and their advancements and influences into our modern times.

No Power in the Verse Can Stop Me!

S. Asher

Made in the USA
Middletown, DE
14 August 2019